TEAMING BY DESIGN:

REAL TEAMS FOR REAL PEOPLE

TEAMING BY DESIGN:
REAL TEAMS FOR REAL PEOPLE

DONNA McINTOSH-FLETCHER

The McFletcher Corporation

IRWIN
Professional Publishing

Chicago • Bogotá • Boston • Buenos Aires • Caracas
London • Madrid • Mexico City • Sydney • Toronto

Portions of this material have been published by Donna McIntosh-Fletcher and the McFletcher Corporation under previous copyright, 1978-1993.

© The McFletcher Corporation, 1996

Irwin Professional Book Team

Senior sponsoring editor: *Cynthia A. Zigmund*
Marketing manager: *Kelly Sheridan*
Production supervisor: *Dina L. Treadaway*
Assistant manager, desktop services: *Jon Christopher*
Project editor: *Beth Cigler*
Designer: *Crispin Prebys*
Cover Designer: *Tim Kaage*
Compositor: *David Corona Design*
Typeface: *11/13 Times Roman*
Printer: *R. R. Donnelley & Sons Company*

Times Mirror
Higher Education Group

Library of Congress Cataloging-in-Publication Data

McIntosh-Fletcher, Donna.
    Teaming by design : real teams for real people / Donna McIntosh
-Fletcher
      p.   cm.
    Includes index.
    ISBN 0–7863–0536–3
    1. Work groups.   I. Title.
HD66.M394   1996
658.4'036—dc20   95–22722

Printed in the United States of America
1 2 3 4 5 6 7 8 9 0 DO 2 1 0 9 8 7 6 5

Dedication and Acknowledgments

To the "real people" who have worked diligently to make "real teams" become a reality:

The McFletcher staff, who leave their egos at the door and with humility learn, live, and work the principles of teaming.

Our clients and colleagues whose Teams in Action *stories are woven throughout the book. Although not identified, they will recognize themselves and their determination to design team processes that make a difference for their organizations.*

My partner Tomas, who has joined me in working with team after team for the past 20 years, creating concepts and exercises that are enlightening and true to the team's work.

The McFletcher writing team, who did whatever it took to get this book out!

Author
Donna McIntosh-Fletcher

Contributors	**Reviewers**	**Text and Graphic Designers**
Judy Barrette	Robert Barnes, M.D.	Carol Haney
Jody Baldwin	Ray Newitt	Jenny Lim
Chris Broderick-Trull	Chris Pappas	Theresa Maggio
W. Thomas (Tomas) McIntosh-Fletcher	Maradell Peters	

From whom the whole body fitly joined together and compacted by that which every joint supplieth, according to the effectual working in the measure of every part, maketh increase of the body unto the edifying of itself in love.

Ephesians 4:16
King James Version

• • •

INTRODUCTION

What is a team? Do we need teams? Where do we need teams? Who belongs on a team? Why are we a team? How can we function better as a team? . . . Sound familiar?

Teaming by Design: Real Teams for Real People answers these questions and more through a systems approach to teams. Complete with definitions, checklists, worksheets, exercises, and true stories of "Teams in Action," this handbook will help you, your co-team members, and your sponsoring organization to:

- Gain basic knowledge about how teams work.
- Develop a system for teaming.
- Apply the steps for starting and developing a team.
- Understand how teams are organized.
- Create a team charter.
- Assess the degree of teaming required.
- Establish team assignments.
- Clarify team support roles.
- Work together productively and cohesively.
- Balance the diverse strengths of team members.
- Hold successful team meetings.

Organizations often mistakenly call existing work groups "teams" or add cross functional representation to a problem-solving group and then assume this is a team. However true teaming depends upon a systematic approach to assessing the need for teams and determining the required level of teaming in an organization. *Teaming by Design: Real Teams for Real People* provides a team process flow for this systematic approach.

Each chapter presents concepts and definitions for team processes, followed by instructions and questions for team members.

At the end of each chapter, a Teams in Action example describes the true story of a team situation in a work setting. It also includes a description of process steps or an exercise the team used for its specific situation. These stories come from a variety of types of organizations including government, industry, small business, and community organizations. The situations include start-up organizations, product teams, manufacturing groups, customer service teams, work groups, and management staff. You and your co-team members can apply the process steps illustrated in the examples to your team situations.

CONTENTS

There are two table of contents formats in this book: (1) a standard listing for easy location of a chapter or topic (see this page) and (2) a 2-page spread to illustrate the scope of the book as well as the process flow for structuring and forming a team (see pages xii and xiii).

CONTENTS

CHAPTER EIGHT

RUNNING TEAM MEETINGS   123

CONTENTS

FLOW AND CONTENTS

TEAMING BY DESIGN:
REAL TEAMS FOR REAL PEOPLE

FLOW AND CONTENTS

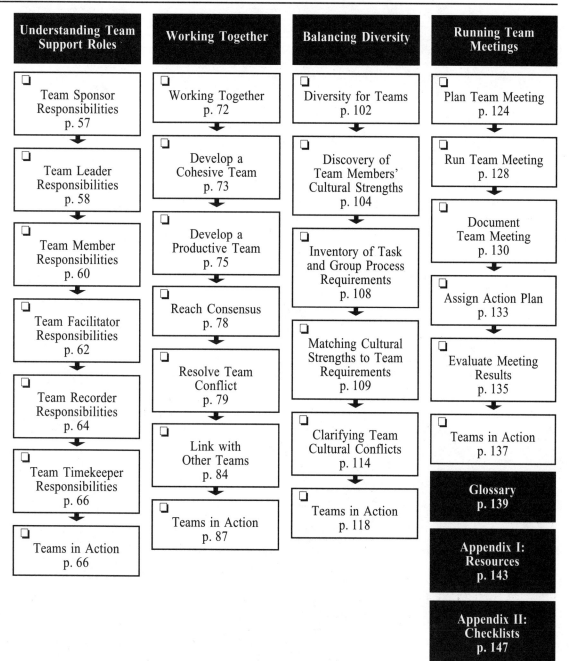

CHAPTER ONE

INTRODUCING TEAMS

he Teams in Action story for this chapter shares the process an American Indian community used to determine its customer base. When the U.S. government realized the Bureau of Indian Affairs needed to shift its focus from controlling to servicing and supporting Indian communities, this tribal administrative team chose to take a proactive stance in providing cross-functional team leadership.

• • •

WHAT IS A TEAM?

Cohesive work groups that also have interdependent tasks and common goals can outproduce and outperform any random collection of individuals. This has been recognized for centuries in many cultures, whether through communities, athletic groups, or social institutions. In the workplace these groups may differ in form, such as semiautonomous teams, multiskilled groups, customer-service units, high-performance-work task forces, or quality-control circles.

A team is commonly defined as several people associated together in work or activity. Yet a more complete definition of the word **team** is "a group of individuals who share work activities and the responsibility for specific outcomes." Team members have inter-dependent work; that is, they need the work of other members to achieve shared goals. Following are three important thoughts to expand upon in the definition:

1. **Interdependence,** in which each team member makes individual contributions. Other members depend on those contributions and share work information with one another. Members are also accepted by and able to influence one another.
2. **Shared responsibility.** Responsibility for the team's purpose and goals is shared and understood by all members (rather than held solely by the manager or team leader).
3. **Outcome,** accountability for **team outcomes** is shared by all members, which identifies the focus for the team's activities and includes both services and products.

Consider your team; is it simply functioning as a cohesive work group or as a team as defined earlier? Is your work interdependent with the work of others? Does your team share responsibility for the **team goals?** Do all members assume accountability for team outcomes?

WHY TEAMS?

Whether structured in the form of groups, teams, or units, an organization is first a collection of people—people working to ensure the success of their organization. Organizations are recognizing the need to encourage people to work collectively and to employ entrepreneurial activity at every level.

Entrepreneurial talent can be used effectively within an organization by establishing accountable work groups in the form of self-directed teams who champion a particular process, product, or cause.

The most productive way for organizations to make large-scale improvements in the way they serve their customers is to involve people from all areas and levels in the organization. Progress cannot be made without utilizing **collective wisdom**—the knowledge, experience, and information of a broad base of people. When people pool their skills, knowledge, and talents, they accomplish more. The synergistic energy of people working together further enhances team success.

Organizations implementing teams are acknowledging three important facts of organizational decision making that support establishing teams in the workplace:

1. Decision making is most effective at the levels where the decisions will be carried out.
2. Those people closest to the work are the best equipped to discover solutions and innovations.
3. People are more committed to supporting what they help create.

Again, consider your team. Are you making decisions together about the work? Are you and your comembers involved in and committed to the success of the team's work?

WHAT TYPES OF TEAMS ARE THERE?

There are two primary classifications of teams: **cross-functional teams** and **intact teams.**

A *cross-functional team* is comprised of members representing various parts of the formal organization thus enabling the team to have multiple focuses. It is common for this type of team to have a specific, one-time assignment that addresses a broad issue, problem, or opportunity. The team's lifetime is defined by completion of the assignment. Its members are "matrixed" or co-located from their primary work area with the team assignment being secondary to the members' primary work. A team leader may be formally assigned, or a team member can be selected from within the group to assume the leadership role.

An *intact team* is a permanent or existing work group that produces an identifiable product or service. It may have a team manager who does not participate as a member but rather provides scheduling and coordinating leadership so the team members can focus exclusively on the direct tasks. Or, the team may have a team leader who performs the duties of a member as well as scheduling, conducting team meetings, and coordinating with groups outside the team. The team leader role is often rotated to develop leadership skills among all the team members.

A mature, self-directing or autonomous intact team functions like a small company. It has business accountabilities and direct contact with suppliers and customers. It is responsible for managing its internal affairs, satisfying its customers, managing its financial performance, and continuously improving productivity. To implement these responsibilities, the team's members must possess a broader base of skills and knowledge than those who have individual assignments, group work, or cross-functional responsibilities.

Figure 1–1, *Types of Teams Matrix,* highlights differences among cross-functional teams, intact teams, and other groups. It also outlines the use of teaming skills within teams and in other group settings. Refer to this matrix to determine the type of team to which you belong.

FIGURE 1–1 TYPES OF TEAMS MATRIX	TEAM TYPE		OTHER GROUPS
	CROSS-FUNCTIONAL TEAMS	**INTACT TEAMS**	**COMMITTEES AND COUNCILS, ETC.**
MEMBERSHIP	Members from more than one function	Members of a natural work group or unit	Members from more than one function
LENGTH OF TIME	Life defined by task completion	Permanent life	Permanent or defined life
OBJECTIVES	Single task focus	Perform tasks within defined boundaries	Coordination of some activity or improvement
MEASURES	Achievement of established task(s) and milestones	Achievement of established organizational goals or objectives	Fulfillment of designated charter
EXAMPLES	Business-improvement teams Supplier partnerships Workplace-improvement teams Problem-solving groups Product-tracking groups Task teams	Manufacturing cells Business teams Product-development groups Work units Integrated-product teams Integrated-service groups	Advisory committees Technical ladder councils Promotion review boards Leadership councils Quality and productivity councils Steering committees

What Are the Goals of Teams?

Every team establishes its own goals. The goals are created to accomplish the team's assignments and to support the organization's mission. Generally speaking, the goals of team efforts can be broken into three parts: (1) to *identify* work processes, solutions, or improvements that will move the team's work closer to the organization's vision; (2) to *make recommendations* for implementing those processes, solutions, or improvements; (3) to *implement* and *validate* the recommendations (assure results). With this three-part method of addressing goals, the team contributes to the organization's continuous efforts towards achievement.

In some cases teams have interdependent goals. One team will pass off its work to another team, which will complete the next part of the work. For example, one team might plan a change for improvement, another team may then be assigned a specific problem to solve so the change can take place, and yet another team may be responsible for implementation. (To create your team goals, see Chapter 3, "Organizing Teams.")

Who Are Team Customers?

It is important to define the term **customer** as used in this book. The end user of a product or service is a customer, but there are also other kinds of customers. The traditional definition of *customer* is one who *purchases* goods, products, or services. The expanded definition of the word *customer* is any person or entity that *uses* goods, products, or services. Customers can be *external* to the organization or other people or teams *within* the organization.

Any time a service, product, piece of paper, form, instruction, or assignment is delivered, an interchange exists with a customer. It is important to remember that customers keep the business in business.

Consider whether your team supplies its customers with what is most needed. Are there services you offer that the customer basically ignores or seldom uses? Are they tossing portions of your product away without using them (e.g., internal status reports)? Are your customers delighted with the product or service, or are they simply accepting what they get? Are the processes your team uses the most effective for making the product or delivering the service?

TEAMS IN ACTION

Figure 1–2, *Teams in Action Example: Who Is the Customer,* provides a list of questions to prompt a team dialog and discovery. The team story, from a progressive and prominent American Indian community that borders a large metropolitan area, illustrates how the questions were used to develop a clear understanding of the team's customer base.

TEAM SITUATION

The management and administrative team for this Indian community initiated leadership training to prepare the community for self- sufficiency from the Bureau of Indian Affairs (BIA) and ultimately the U.S. Government. The tribal council had delegated this responsibility to the team in preparation for anticipated congressional changes of reduced BIA control over the management of American Indian communities. This possibly represented the most significant opportunity in over 100 years for the American Indians to determine their community's destiny. Therefore, this team needed to gain clarity about its customer base to maintain a clear focus and to refrain from getting sidetracked. Was the customer base the BIA, the Tribal Leadership Council, or the members of the community?

The team also faced expectations and pressures from external entities such as neighboring cities, the State Department of Transportation, farmers, and commercial developers, all of whom perceived themselves as customers. These were entities who wanted to plan and collaborate with the team to gain access to the Indian land for roads, water rights, and commercial development. But were they customers, suppliers, partners, or competitors?

TEAM PROCESSES

The questions listed in the Teams in Action example were used to obtain clarity about the team's customer base. The team members used the process steps listed below to assess the various entities.

Process Steps:

1. Conduct surveys with the questions.
2. Review historical records.
3. Interview key individuals.
4. Document and review all the information gathered.
5. Identify primary customer, other customers, and end users.

FIGURE 1-2
TEAMS IN ACTION
EXAMPLE

WHO IS THE CUSTOMER?

Products/Services

1. What products or services have we delivered over the past five years and to whom?

2. Are there any trends we can see over the past year? Two years? Five years?

3. How many of the products/services were repeatedly provided to the same individuals/groups/organizations?

4. What requests for products/services has our team received and to which have we not responded?

Clients/Customers

5. What is the profile of our typical client/customer (for example, types of individuals, groups, or products lines; manufacturing, service, or government organization; size of operation—local to worldwide)?

6. How pleased are our clients/customers with what we do? What means do we have to know how well our products/services are being utilized or received?

7. Do we depend on other functions or teams to help us in the delivery of our products/services? To what extent do we depend on them or they on us? What are these functions or teams? How good are our working relationships?

Financial Factors

8. From whom is the greatest distribution of our costs or profits? Do we have an even distribution of revenue from our clients/customers (or is 20 percent of the total number of clients/customers typically providing 80 percent of the revenue)? To whom should we dedicate time and give the most attention?

9. What financial factors are most likely to affect the delivery of our products/services and who our customers will be? (For example, corporate changes and shifting priorities, capital investments or improvements, labor costs, economic conditions, etc.)

Changes or Issues

10. What changes or issues are most likely to affect our client(s)/customer(s) and thus change their demand for our services? (For example, population shifts, technological improvements, work process changes, employment opportunities, education shifts, interest rates, leisure demands, inflation changes, political positions, environmental concerns, etc.)

11. Will these changes or issues create new customers or cause a shift in those we have now?

Team Results

The exercise of posing the questions for fact finding was not easy, as the external entities had been customers to this community through the BIA for a number of years. The team decided the Tribal Leadership Council would need to be its primary customer, with the community members at large as the ultimate customer—or end users. The team developed educational and intervention strategies to inform everyone of decisions made and to resolve potential conflicts between the council and the community members. It also determined ways to select the best external entities for partnering with the community. These entities represented the resources for questions 8 and 9, which addressed financial factors.

The team facilitated the community in collaborative land development projects. This resulted in the development of one of the most active and profitable shopping centers in the area, while keeping the vast majority of the land for the community members to farm. The team also negotiated with several hundred of the community members to enable the tribal council to obtain rights to the land. The team then helped to facilitate a council interface with the State Department of Transportation to sell a long strip of the outer edge of the community to the state for a future freeway. The shopping center development and the sale of land provided a large flow of money to the council for community development and to the community members for self development.

CHAPTER TWO

❏ Suggested Steps
    p. 9

❏ Teams in Action
    p. 17

DEVELOPING TEAMWORK

The Teams in Action *story for "Developing Teamwork" includes the management team of a county social service agency. They used the* Checklist for a Productive Team *provided in this chapter as a means to have a frank discussion regarding their trust and mistrust issues. Just as they were posting their results (which were not necessarily ones to advertise) the State Director of Social Services arrived for a surprise visit.*

• • •

SUGGESTED STEPS

For a team to be successful it must become a productive unit. To be productive, a team must target goals and achieve those goals in the most efficient way possible. The following suggested steps will help you develop a productive team:

1. Identify the need for a team and the degree of teaming required.
2. Get to know one another and utilize team strengths.
3. Form a team charter.

4. Identify and perform team tasks to support the charter.
5. Use creative and analytical team tools.
6. Work together, reach consensus, and resolve conflicts.
7. Cooperate with other teams and the larger organization.
8. Evaluate the team's productivity and cohesiveness.
9. Make recommendations for action.
10. Celebrate team success.

This chapter of the book provides an overview of the steps to develop teamwork. Guidelines for how to do the steps are in the chapters that follow.

1. IDENTIFY THE NEED

The organization and/or the team must determine whether a team is needed. Look at the situation and assess whether it is a shared problem to be solved or a process to be improved. Is it a staff function, production operation, or work situation that requires interdependent work activities? Then ask, can an individual or existing department do the work? Is a team needed to do this work or assignment? If so, how much teaming is required, do individuals work independently at times and in team at times, or is all work done in team? (See Chapters 3 and 4 "Organizing the Team" and "Assessing Team Requirements" for techniques in determining the degree of teaming required.)

Once it has been decided that a team is needed, and the extent of teaming required has been assessed, determine what types of team member skills, experience, knowledge, and attributes are required to perform the work. Before selecting team members, consider what size the team should be to effectively conduct the work. Problem solving and decision making work best in teams of five to nine people. With fewer than five people, teams do not have enough input and viewpoints; with more than nine, teams have trouble reaching consensus.

2. KNOW ONE ANOTHER

It is important to get to know one another early in the team effort. Learn about one another's talents, interests, work background and preferences so that you can use each member as a valuable resource.

Often, specific culturally based skills are not considered, and when team members share what they have to offer, it is from a narrow band of thinking such as work experience or education. The sharing of cultural experiences such as family life or heritage develops a deeper level of appreciation.

By valuing and understanding differences, mutual respect and trust are gained. Suggestions for how to get to know one another are provided in three chapters of this book: "Organizing Teams," "Working Together," and "Balancing Diversity."

3. FORM TEAM CHARTER

The team charter consists of the team's mission or purpose, goals and objectives, team role, and guidelines. A clear charter keeps the team focused on its mission and goals. Once agreed upon, the team's energy is directed toward achieving the goals set forth in the charter.

No changes in the team's charter or goals should be made unless absolutely necessary and only with the full agreement and support of the team, including the team leader and the team sponsor. (See Chapter 3, "Organizing the Team," for a more complete description of the contents of the charter.)

4. PERFORM TEAM TASKS

To achieve the team's goals, each team will have important tasks to perform. Some of these are:

- Identifying and completing action items.
- Planning work assignments.
- Communicating efforts and decisions.
- Identifying and finding resources.
- Presenting to one another and to others outside the team.
- Linking with other teams and the larger organization.

Figure 2–1, *Assignment Planning Checklist for Teams,* will help your team develop good planning habits. Refer to Chapters 6 and 8, "Working Together" and "Running Meetings," for more information about performing team tasks.

FIGURE 2-1

ASSIGNMENT PLANNING CHECKLIST FOR TEAMS*†

When Planning Work Assignments with Other Team Members, Do We:	No	Yes Sometimes	Yes Consistently
1. Specify the assignment's main **purpose?**	❏	❏	❏
2. Stress the **results** we need following completion of each assignment?	❏	❏	❏
3. Determine how the **work assignment** fits with other work being done?	❏	❏	❏
4. Clarify how the **assignment** may or may not be different from previous assignments?	❏	❏	❏
5. Provide all the **information** needed to successfully carry out the assignment?	❏	❏	❏
6. List answers to the **"what, when, who, where, how, and why"** of the assignment?	❏	❏	❏
7. Assess the **limitations** (e.g., time, cost, etc.) that could affect the assignment's completion?	❏	❏	❏
8. Provide for **contingencies** or alternate plans should difficulties arise?	❏	❏	❏
9. Reinforce **critical parts** of the assignment by checking on our work in progress and giving positive feedback?	❏	❏	❏
10. Establish **controls** with each other so we're checking on progress?	❏	❏	❏
11. **Document** our plans, process, and results for group memory and shared accountability?	❏	❏	❏
12. Arrange for **coordination** with other departments or teams who might be affected by the work assignment?	❏	❏	❏
13. Solicit **feedback** from team members to assess our shared understanding of the assignment?	❏	❏	❏
14. Arrange for **reviewing/debriefing** after the assignment is completed?	❏	❏	❏

* This checklist is located in Appendix II: Checklists.

† Use this checklist as a preplanning guideline to help clarify assignments and avoid duplication.

5. Use Team Tools

To do their work, teams need to be familiar with an array of tools such as the following:

- Check sheet
- Flow chart
- Interview
- Fish bone diagram
- Gantt chart
- Force field analysis
- Pareto chart
- Histogram
- Control chart

Books and instruction guidelines on these tools are available in public and company libraries. Quality and human resource functions within companies may offer training and processes for these tools. There are also suppliers who have training materials for these tools, such as Zenger Miller and the American Supplier Institute (ASI). (See "Appendix I: Resources" and "Glossary" for more information on suppliers.)

6. Work Together

Teamwork implies working together for the common goal. This requires give-and-take on everyone's part. In order for a team to possess mutual trust and support, it is essential that all team members feel membership—a sense of belonging—with the team and that they feel they have influence within the team.

Reaching consensus and resolving conflicts are crucial to achieving effective teamwork. Team members are frequently confused about consensus. Some mistakenly think it means everyone must end up agreeing with everyone else. They may be understandably apprehensive about being expected to achieve consensus, especially on topics and issues of longstanding concern and disagreement.

Consensus is reached when everyone can support a team decision 100 percent. When conflict is involved, reaching consensus is a win–win solution: everyone can accept the decision, and no one has to abandon any strongly held conviction or need.

Conflict is a natural part of teamwork. In fact, attempts to avoid conflict can even backfire and cause more conflict. It is important, therefore, that team leaders, facilitators, and members deal with conflict in a healthy and constructive way. Some conflict can and should be avoided, while other conflict needs to be understood and resolved creatively.

Chapter 6, "Working Together," offers basic information for developing a healthy and productive team. It also provides suggestions for reaching consensus and resolving conflict.

7. Cooperate with Other Teams

In organizations, teams need to collaborate and cooperate with other teams, not compete. Team recommendations need to be integrated into the larger organization. In addition to keeping others informed, collaborating with other teams when appropriate, and giving presentations, your team will want to influence the implementation of its ideas. This requires a close working relationship with those teams who will be carrying out the work of your team. (See Chapters 4, 6, and 7, "Assessing Team Requirements," "Working Together," and "Balancing Diversity".)

8. Evaluate Teamwork

A productive team takes responsibility for evaluating its productivity and cohesiveness. From time to time the team members can ask basic questions about how they are working together as a team:

- Are we focused on our goals?
- Are we making progress toward those goals?
- Are our meetings productive? Why? Why not?
- Do we faithfully keep to the guidelines we established in the charter? Do we need to amend those guidelines?
- Do we have the resources we need?

Figure 2–2, *Checklist for a Productive Team,* can be completed by team members and discussed as a team. This checklist will help the team identify areas of strength and areas for improvement.

Keep the following guidelines in mind when using the checklist to evaluate your team's productivity:

FIGURE 2-2

CHECKLIST FOR A PRODUCTIVE TEAM*†

Please refer to this "Extent Scale Guide" in answering the following questions:

	Very Little Extent	Little Extent	Some Extent	Great Extent	Very Great Extent
1. To what extent do you enjoy performing your team activities?	1	2	3	4	5
2. To what extent do you feel a real responsibility to help your team be successful?	1	2	3	4	5
3. To what extent do you feel you are accepted as a member of your team?	1	2	3	4	5
4. To what extent do you feel you receive enough praise or recognition when a job is well done?	1	2	3	4	5
5. How receptive are people higher in the organization to team suggestions and new ideas?	1	2	3	4	5
6. Does the organization keep an open and frank flow of information about important events affecting your team?	1	2	3	4	5
7. Do other functions or teams plan and coordinate their efforts to maintain an effective flow of work activity?	1	2	3	4	5
8. Are there things about working on this team (people, policies, or conditions) that encourage you to work hard?	1	2	3	4	5
9. To what extent is the organization generally quick to accept your team's improved work methods?	1	2	3	4	5
10. Are the decisions made at those levels where the most adequate and accurate information is available?	1	2	3	4	5
11. Does the organization have a real interest in the welfare and happiness of those who work on your team?	1	2	3	4	5
12. How much does the organization try to improve working conditions for your team?	1	2	3	4	5
13. To what extent does the organization have clear-cut, reasonable goals and objectives for your team to support?	1	2	3	4	5
14. To what extent are work activities for this team sensibly organized?	1	2	3	4	5
15. How adequate is the information you get about other functions (or related teams)?	1	2	3	4	5
16. Are the equipment and resources your team has to work with adequate, efficient, and well maintained?	1	2	3	4	5

Adapted and modified for teams from Organization Dynamics, Inc., 1978.

* This checklist is located in Appendix II: Checklists.

† This checklist can be completed by team members and discussed as a team.

- Do use it for learning and correction purposes.
- Do use it as a feedback tool to help your team continuously improve its effectiveness.
- Do use it to help you and your co-team members credit yourselves for doing well.
- Do not use it to single out, criticize, or joke about any team member.
- Do not use it to judge others or to judge the team's performance.

Chapters 5 and 6, "Understanding Team Roles" and "Working Together," provide a variety of concepts and checklists for more specific guidelines in evaluating your team's effectiveness.

9. RECOMMENDATIONS FOR ACTION

To be effective, a team needs to agree on recommendations for action and marshal support from appropriate places in the organization. Often teams will make a recommendation for action in a presentation and a written report. This is one of the most important steps your team will take, and the entire team should become involved in the preparation process.

Chapter 8, "Running Team Meetings," provides ways to document your team recommendations and decisions. Chapter 6, "Working Together," suggests ways to link with other parts of the organization for both marshaling and providing support.

10. CELEBRATE

A little bit of fun can go a long way! One advantage to being on a team is the camaraderie; others are there to "share your concerns" and to "share your successes." As identified by recent research on high-tech work environments, loneliness and isolation are frequent employee complaints. In team environments, however, group activities and celebrations can be reinstituted.

Remember that when celebrating, simple things often mean more than elaborate awards. Some suggestions for celebrating team success are

- Potluck lunches.
- Afternoon ball games.
- Viewing movies with popcorn—even educational movies.
- Friday afternoon socials.
- Dress or casual days for certain events.
- Releasing balloons to symbolize completion.
- Fortune cookies with thank-you notes.

TEAMS IN ACTION

A county social service agency had been selected by the State Department of Social Services to conduct a pilot organization-development program. The purpose of this pilot was exploring different ways to provide and manage services that would benefit the state through reduced costs while also providing increased services for welfare recipients.

TEAM SITUATION

This particular county agency was selected for the pilot because it needed a turnaround in its performance and it had a new director with a reputation for being an innovative and effective leader. But he was not succeeding in obtaining his management staff's buy-in of the program. The staff did not even consider themselves a team, as he had assumed they should. Most of the staff members had been with the agency for a number of years and had become either indifferent or hostile in their attitudes toward their work in general and particularly toward change. The employees in the agency who reported to this team were also resistant. This was puzzling to the new director, so he scheduled a three-day retreat for the management team in order to obtain their support and cooperation and to plan the pilot program. Unknown to the team, he also invited the State Director of Social Services to visit during the retreat to relay some program highlights. He hoped that this surprise visit would motivate and inspire the team.

TEAM PROCESS

There was little group cohesion or interest during the first day of the retreat. In fact most of the members played cards until the wee hours of the morning and were too tired to concentrate during the day. On the morning of the second day, before the new director arrived, the retreat facilitators confronted the team, addressing their lack of participation. The team members explained that past efforts to improve things had only caused more work. They had also experienced repercussions from their past director when they attempted to be honest about work errors and agency issues. And finally, they admitted they distrusted this new "hot shot" director.

The facilitators suggested using the *Checklist for a Productive Team* (see Figure 2–2) as a dialog tool. They assured the group that their input would be confidential. The managers responded positively to this idea; they saw it as a way to show their new director some truths about the agency. No one knew that the new director was late to the session because he was picking up the State Director at the airport.

The team used the process steps listed below to do the assessment and dialog. (See Figure 2–3 for team results).

Process Steps:

1. Each individual completes the checklists in private and writes reasons for each selected extent score. (Allow up to one hour for individual thinking and writing.)
2. Keep the checklists anonymous for confidentiality and give them to a facilitator to tabulate the results on large easel paper or on an overhead as illustrated in Figure 2–3. (Optional: show the number of responses for each category on the scale and discuss openly who placed their response where and why. This eliminates confidentiality and should be used to build trust in teams where openness is necessary for the nature of the work or when team members are ready for this level of sharing.)
3. Conduct a team dialog for each checklist question:
   Review the range of responses.

   Discuss reasons for the Very Little Extent and Very Great Extent selections; then discuss the middle range, Little to Great Extent, selections.
4. Record on a separate easel sheet team members' reasons for their extent rating for each question.
5. Allow time for "dumping" and sharing; use this as a healing process.

FIGURE 2-3
TEAMS IN ACTION EXAMPLE

SOCIAL SERVICE MANAGEMENT TEAM CHECKLIST FOR A PRODUCTIVE TEAM

Please refer to this "Extent Scale Guide" in answering the following questions:

Very Little Extent	Little Extent	Some Extent	Great Extent	Very Great Extent

1. To what extent do you enjoy performing your team activities?

1 — 2   3   4   5
not rewarding

2. To what extent do you feel a real responsibility to help your team be successful?

1 — 2 — 3   4   5
no one supports. me

3. To what extent do you feel you are accepted as a member of your team?

1 — 2 — 3 — 4 — 5
some never / some greatly

4. To what extent do you feel you receive enough praise or recognition when a job is well done?

1 — 2   3   4   5
not invented here

5. How receptive are people higher in the organization to team suggestions and new ideas?

1   2 — 3 — 4   5
the new guy — yes

6. Does the organization keep an open and frank flow of information about important events affecting your team?

1 — 2   3   4 — 5
some out   some in

7. Do other functions or teams plan and coordinate their efforts to maintain an effective flow of work activity?

1 — 2 — 3   4   5
who has time?

8. Are there things about working on this team (people, policies, or conditions) that encourage you to work hard?

1   2   3 — 4 — 5
the clients

9. To what extent is the organization generally quick to accept your team's improved work methods?

1   2 — 3 — 4   5
maybe now

10. Are the decisions made at those levels where the most adequate and accurate information is available?

1 — 2 — 3   4   5
never

11. Does the organization have a real interest in the welfare and happiness of those who work on your team?

1 — 2 — 3   4   5
not much

12. How much does the organization try to improve working conditions for your team?

1   2 — 3 — 4   5
beginning to

13. To what extent does the organization have clear-cut, reasonable goals and objectives for your team to support?

1 — 2 — 3   4   5
state direction keeps changing

14. To what extent are work activities for this team sensibly organized?

1   2 — 3   4   5
no choice

15. How adequate is the information you get about other functions (or related teams)?

1 — 2 — 3   4   5
off and on

16. Are the equipment and resources your team has to work with adequate, efficient, and well maintained?

1 — 2 — 3 — 4   5
mostly old / phones new — yes

Adapted and modified for teams from Organization Dynamics, Inc., 1978

6. Problem solve and create an action plan:

> Great to Very Great Extent—areas of strengths: Plan how to reinforce and maintain these strengths.

> Little to Very Little Extent—areas of weakness: Use problem-solving steps to determine root causes versus symptoms, and plan corrective actions.

TEAM RESULTS

A frank two-hour discussion occurred in which some heart-wrenching realities were shared. The team's results were posted along with the reasons. Only 3 of the 16 questions received a Very Great Extent rating—and only by those individuals perceived as favored by the new director. As the group began discussing how this happened, the two directors arrived. Some team members tried to distract the directors while the facilitators discreetly moved the easel sheets. However, the new director observed what was happening and used the opportunity to work openly with the group. He requested that the team share their results with him and the State Director. They shared the process but discussed the checklist results selectively and cautiously.

After the State Director left, the team openly presented what had transpired, as well as all of their checklist results, to the County Director. They felt comfortable taking this risk due to their director's willingness to receive the unflattering information in the presence of his boss.

Over the next two years this agency embarked upon a total restructuring of attitudes, policies, procedures, and positions under the leadership of this management team. It was not easy, but it worked and people from all levels of the organization said it made a difference—the agency became a great place to work. The tenth step in developing teams was enacted with a department-wide luncheon to celebrate their success.

During their celebration, the director announced that the state had reviewed their program and established a statewide social service improvement committee to institute elements of the program with other county agencies. During this time, the state was recognized as a model state in welfare benefits and services by the U.S. Department of Health, Education, and Welfare. This pilot program was part of the recognized model.

CHAPTER THREE

ORGANIZING THE TEAM

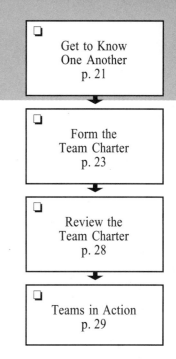

❑ Get to Know
One Another
p. 21

❑ Form the
Team Charter
p. 23

❑ Review the
Team Charter
p. 28

❑ Teams in Action
p. 29

*T*he Teams in Action *story that closes this chapter describes a cross-functional committee that established three agencywide teams for a state department of transportation. The design and implementation of a comprehensive career system was their three-year goal. At the time of this writing they are in their second year. Keeping all 61 team members from all parts of the state motivated and involved through the project's completion was their challenge. Creating their charter with team goals and designation of interteam objectives is illustrated.*

• • •

GET TO KNOW ONE ANOTHER

Spend time getting to know one another at the first team meeting. One way to do this is to post a few questions for each person to answer, then go around the room giving each person a few minutes to introduce him or herself and answer the questions.

Sample Questions:

- What is your name and current role/assignment?
- What other assignments or work experiences have you held?
- What particular skills do you have?
- What is a favorite thing you have done on a job?
- A least favorite thing?
- What makes work worthwhile for you?
- In what ways will you be able to contribute to this team?

Use various icebreakers at subsequent meetings until the team members seem comfortable with one another. In the icebreakers, you can include information about people's hobbies, likes and dislikes, former careers, favorite vacation spots, and so forth.

Getting to know one another more fully can be accomplished with assessment inventories. The McFletcher Corporation's *Work-Style Patterns Inventory™ (WSP™)* is a self-scoring assessment tool to use with teams. It helps clarify individual preferences and determine what makes work worthwhile for individual members. It also compares the alignment and stress levels between preferred and required WorkStyles. Have each member of the team complete the *WorkStyle Patterns™ Inventory (WSP™)* to determine team members' preferences and to identify the most productive ways to assign team tasks.

The *WSP™* and behavioral inventories such as the *Myers–Briggs Type Indicator® (MBTI®), LIFO®,* and the *Personal Profile System© (DISC)* complement each other. These behavioral inventories can be used separately for their unique assessment or in conjunction with the *WSP™* for additional depth of understanding. Use the *WSP™* for team development with individual and group WorkStyle preferences and for clarification of work requirements. Use the behavioral inventories for team building with individual and group behavior types.

Once the initial team membership has been established, you will need to have a shared understanding as to the purpose of your team. Forming a **team charter** together is a great way to do this. It takes time to do, but it saves time and prevents confusion in the long run.

FORM THE TEAM CHARTER

A simplified version of a team charter consists of the following:

The team **mission,** or **purpose,** identifies why the team exists. It sets the boundaries for what will and will not be done. The team mission supports the organization's vision. The vision conveys the values, direction, and meaning of individual and collective effort. Some mission statements include aspects of a vision.

Mission addresses why the team exists.

Goals are specific targets that will bring the team closer to realizing its mission. These are established for a specific time frame such as one year or five years.

Goals address what the team is going to do.

Objectives are the actions that support the goals. They are the who, what, how, where, and when—expressed in percentages, time frames, proportions, and other measurements. Stated objectives include the resources required to achieve the objectives. They are subject to change and revision.

Objectives address how the team is going to meet the goals.

The **team role** is the part the team plays in helping the organization meet its vision. This identifies the approach the team needs to meet its own purpose, goals, and objectives and to support the organization's mission.

Team role identifies the work approach the team should assume as a group.

Guidelines are the ground rules or norms for how a team will do its work and how members will behave with one another.

Guidelines are the team norms that specify team processes; they designate how the team will work together.

TEAM MISSION/PURPOSE

To determine the team's purpose, list key reasons why the organization needs this team:

_____

_____

_____

_____

_____

_____

_____

Form this into a mission statement (using reasons from above):

The _____ *team's mission is to*
      (name of team)

_____

_____

_____

_____

_____

_____

_____

GOALS AND OBJECTIVES

Goals serve as a means to focus the energies of those who are affected by the goals and those who need to make them happen. Goals will change more frequently than philosophy/mission/purpose statements and, in turn, are more subject to technical, economic, social, political, and other forces both within and outside the organization.

Goal statements reflect more specific targets to bring the team closer to realizing its mission. Example:

> *A team goal is to increase our market share in the hospitality industry next year.*

Objectives refine goal statements and are concrete, expressing percentages, time frames, proportions, and so forth. They include the resources required to achieve the goals. Objectives are used best when reviewed and updated regularly. Example:

> *Next year's market share in hospitality sales will increase from 16 to 22 percent in the southeast region.*

A sample format to use for setting the team goals and objectives is illustrated in Figure 3–1.

FIGURE 3–1

GOALS AND OBJECTIVES CHECKLIST*		
Team Goal	**Objectives to Support the Goal**	**Target Date for Completion**
1	• • • •	
2	• • • •	
3	• • • •	

* This checklist is located in Appendix II: Checklists.

Teams have different purposes and activities depending upon what the organization most needs from the team, just as assignments in organizations differ according to the needs of the work. Assessing the team's role in the organization will help clarify team members' understanding of the team's purpose and identify the necessary activities.

People often expect a team experience to be similar to past team assignments. When expectations about how the team role supports the mission are not clarified, team members can go about the work with different perceptions. This leads to confusion, which often escalates in misunderstandings and unnecessary conflict among team members. The *Team Model* illustrated in Figure 3–2 shows a three-step process for aligning perceptions of teamwork.

FIGURE 3–2

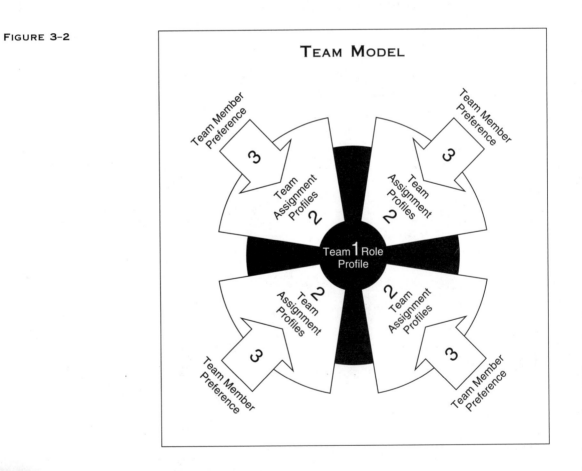

1. Establish the overall role the team should assume to support the team's mission.
2. Determine the approach required in the various team tasks or assignments.
3. Match individuals' preferences to the assignments.

Ways to address Step 1 are provided in the following pages of this chapter. Steps 2 and 3 are discussed in Chapter 6, "Working Together." When doing the first step of the *Team Model,* it's important that all members share the same perception of how the team will meet its mission. Discuss ways the mission might be carried out by the team:

- In a technical mode performing expert work?
- As a strategic group planning for the future?
- As analysts appraising a situation?
- As a group coordinating a set of activities being performed by others?
- In a teaching approach to assure learnings are transferred?

A one-hour discussion and clarification of the role using the questions above may be sufficient if your team has a short-term or part-time assignment. Short-term assignments usually last three months or less. If your team has a long-term assignment or a concentrated short-term assignment that could impact the organization greatly, this discussion can be made easier and more meaningful by administering The McFletcher Corporation's *WorkStyle Patterns™ Team Role Assessment Inventory.*

The *Team Role Assessment Inventory* indicates the WorkStyle approach the organization needs from the team as a whole. The results of the team's assessment will answer the questions above and provide a team WorkStyle™ profile description as well. (See Appendix I: Resources for more information about this inventory.)

ESTABLISH TEAM GUIDELINES

While your team is getting acquainted and beginning its work, it will be informally or formally setting its own guidelines or ground rules for working together. Some people refer to these as team norms.

It is a good idea to discuss and decide upon important team guidelines early on (at one of the first meetings). These can be posted at the team's meetings to remind team members of the agreed upon guidelines. From time to time it may be necessary to review the guidelines and ask:

How well are we keeping to the guidelines we established?

Do we want to add or delete any guidelines?

Common Team Guidelines (Norms)

- Hear one another out.

- When confused, ask.

- Avoid harboring hidden agendas; speak out.

- OK to disagree, but not OK to discount or put others down.

- Build upon one another's ideas.

- Recognize one another for contributions each adds to the team.

- Assist one another when needed.

- Facilitate consensus by offering suggestions rather than criticizing.

- Communicate openly and frequently with one another.

Warning: Do not copy your guidelines from a book or another team. There will be little buy-in and support of them this way. Instead, each team should discuss and decide upon its own guidelines. The team should reach a consensus on each guideline and then honor the guidelines by posting them, referring to them, and pointing out when the team is falling short of them.

REVIEW TEAM CHARTER

After establishing the charter, summarize the strengths and vulnerabilities of your team.

- What strengths or characteristics does your team have that will make it possible to honor its guidelines?

- Do you see any areas for improvement or ways the team composition might be lacking necessary capabilities?

- Are there reasons why the team might not be as effective as it could be?

- Identify how your team will meet its goals and objectives:

    Report completed tasks. Identify to whom to report.

    Communicate between work sessions or meetings.

    Accomplish tasks that involve more than one person.

    Get feedback on tasks they have completed.

    Provide feedback to others in a timely manner.

    Keep information channels open.

- Make sure your team and team members have the commensurate authority and role clarity to carry out the work.

- Plan ways to *immediately* bring work problems to the attention of the team leader or other members, rather than waiting until the next team session or meeting to address those concerns.

TEAM SITUATION

A state agency steering committee was given a three-year assignment to create and assure the implementation of a statewide career system for the agency's 4,500 employees. This committee chose to work as a cross-functional team and followed the processes discussed throughout this chapter to determine the team's purpose and to develop the team charter. The team named itself F.O.C.E.S.— Future Organization Career and Education Strategies. (The committee's *Teams in Action Example: Creating Team Charter* is illustrated in Figure 3–3.)

TEAMS IN ACTION

FIGURE 3-3
TEAMS IN ACTION EXAMPLE

CREATING TEAM CHARTER

DATE: 10/5/93	**Team I.D.**	Career Systems—Future Organization Career and Education Strategies—F.O.C.E.S.

Type of Team Sponsor Level	Vision Supported:
☐ BPI ☑ EQC ☐ TASK ☐ QIC ☐ DUIT ☐ PARTNERING ☐ OEG (formerly SLIM) ☑ OTHER COMMITTEE	# _____✔_____ Guiding Vision # _____ Supplier Partnerships # _____ Customer Relationships # _____ Management Support and Leadership # _____ Business, Products and Service Processes

The Situation/Background: (Statement of situation or problem)	This agency does not currently have an agencywide career development system that is responsive to agency and employee needs and that promotes professional growth and development.

Team Mission: (Purpose)	The Career Development Committee for Future Organization Career and Education Strategies is dedicated to create the vision and provide the general framework; to support, monitor, and guide the implementation of an agencywide career development system.

Team Role WorkStyle Profile:	PROMOTER w/ APPRAISER—"advocate alternatives and manage information."

Accept responsibility for determining alternatives and convincing others of viable options.	Document concerns and recommendations for consideration by others.

Goals and Objectives:	THE F.O.C.E.S.—6

Establish team process: • charter • roles
Data gathering: • benchmarking • surveys • assessments • review of baselines
Integration: • establishing linkages • sharing resources/information • developing contacts
   • F.O.C.E.S. action plan/scope
Program Design: • develop principles • plan programs/services/models • conduct prototype/pilots • implement
Documentation/Presentation: • progress notes • events • evaluation
Monitor/Measure: • conduct evaluations • revise/update

Strategies to Define the Process:	3 focus areas: • Skills development and certification • Leadership and mentoring • Career pathing and mentoring

– Marketing to employees and management – Surveys and data gathering – How system is implemented as a whole	– Packaging – Gantt chart; milestones; flowcharts – Brainstorming	– Career Development committee

Guidelines/Norms: (Team Methods of Conduct)	– start and end on time – be visionary – challenge – focus on areas we can influence – meet timelines	– work toward a common goal – avoid demotivating behaviors – be open-minded

TEAM PROCESS

The F.O.C.E.S. committee realized that it was embarking on an ambitious long-term effort. They decided to create their charter in small steps while also working on their team assignment. This process took three months during which they used the guidelines of this chapter as shown in the process steps listed below.

Process Steps:

1. **Obtain information.**

   Before drafting the mission, the committee members brought in guest speakers on the subject, interviewed state personnel executives, and reviewed existing agency career initiatives. They used this information to write a statement describing the situation.

2. **Establish the mission.**

   Next, they focused on the mission for the Charter. The team used a combination of total group brainstorming and small group assignments to clarify the mission.

3. **Determine team role.**

   The F.O.C.E.S. committee members administered the *WorkStyle Team Role Inventory* as a means to test their shared understanding of the mission statement. They conducted a group dialog regarding their selected activity statements. This dialog provided additional information for their charter.

4. **Develop team goals and objectives.**

   Six career system goals, the F.O.C.E.S.—6, were established by the committee for the teams and other individuals assigned to help with the project. Objectives for each of the F.O.C.E.S.—6 were identified along with strategies or methods to use to reach the goals. One strategy was an integrated Gantt chart with all team activities reflected. This served as the shared planning tool for the entire project. It was also used to assure coordination between teams and to avoid activity overlap. For example, two of the teams had planned to benchmark the same company. This was noted during the Gantt charting process; thus, instead of making two separate visits, both teams' representatives toured the company together.

5. Identify team guidelines/norms.

This committee identified their productive operating and behavioral norms as well as those that were not productive. They then established guidelines for working together and for monitoring their team behavior.

TEAM RESULTS

F.O.C.E.S. is in its second year. The committee has designed and coordinated a comprehensive systems approach for the statewide career system.

It established three teams with specific areas of responsibilities. The members from each of these teams received team training and followed the steps to create their own charters. They also designated team names to identify their primary area of responsibility: Skills-R-Us, Career Pathing, and L.E.A.D. The three team leaders meet with the committee quarterly, and all team members—61 line employees—meet twice a year for shared training and activity linkage.

The F.O.C.E.S. team's success in involving employees to design a career system that is both comprehensive and progressive has led to the state's personnel office decision to use the F.O.C.E.S. model as a pilot. The state personnel office has also assigned a liaison to assist the Skills-R-Us team in identifying skill groupings to include in the state's new classification system.

CHAPTER FOUR

ASSESSING TEAM REQUIREMENTS

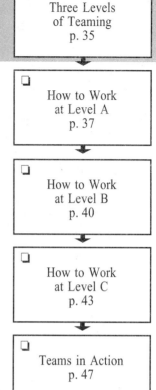

*T*he Teams in Action *story at the close of this chapter tells about a new start-up subsidiary in a Fortune 500 company. This division has become a U.S. Industry/Department of Defense model for Integrated Product Development (IPD) teaming. With vision and courage, the people behind this success "plowed" their way through challenges and barriers to create a work culture for the future. Learn how they assessed the degree of teaming they needed to perform and how they used the same assessment to develop team hiring and selection methods.*

• • •

Over the past 40 years there has been a growing need for cooperation and collaboration in the workplace. Organizations have become more diversified, technology has become increasingly integrated, and information is being processed instantaneously on a global level. The variety and quantity of work that people do has increased, requiring greater task integration and a clearer understanding of worldwide issues.

This movement has changed how organizations structure the concept of working together. Prior to 1960, most work was performed by individuals who were specialists in their particular work.

Although they may have worked alongside other people, their work was not interdependent with the work of others. During the 1970s, the concept of basic group work surfaced with group cooperation and shared information. The productivity issues of the 1980s led to the development of self-directed and autonomous teams. The integration of the massive amounts of information that is readily available to us in the 1990s requires organizations to adapt an even broader concept—that of shared teaming. Shared teaming involves not only integrating team members' work, but also linking the work of the team with other teams and other parts of the organization.

Establishing teams solely because it is a current business trend is not enough to justify the additional effort, process changes, and learning that must occur for teams to be effective. Teams are necessary when the work requires interfacing activities that cannot be accomplished as effectively by individuals.

It is important to understand how the shift to teaming impacts the way work needs to be performed. This chapter addresses two means for assessing teamwork requirements: (1) *Three Levels of Teaming* and (2) *WorkStyle Patterns™ data.*

- The **Three Levels of Teaming** is an assessment process used to determine the degree of teaming required. You and your team members can review the levels presented in this chapter to determine which level of teaming is required to effectively meet your team's mission and role.
- **WorkStyle Patterns™ data** reveal trends for each of the three levels of teaming. These data are presented for you and your co-team members to use when considering current and future work requirements for your team.

  WorkStyle findings are based on data from the *WorkStyle Patterns™ (WSP™) Inventory,* which assesses and compares personal and position WorkStyles. It describes work activities, determines individual preferences, identifies alignment, and compares personal and organizational stress.

  This inventory distinguishes among four WorkStyle Orientations: Task, Project, Organization, and Adapting. The *29 WorkStyle Patterns™ Profiles* use the combination of activities within an orientation to provide more specific information about how a person wants to carry out work activities and the approach that a position or team assignment requires.

Use the information in this chapter to carefully assess the degree of teaming required for your team and your organization. Determine how much and what parts of the work need to be done by teams and compare this with how much and what parts of the work should be done by individuals.

THREE LEVELS OF TEAMING

The *Three Levels of Teaming* are illustrated in Figure 4–1. Level A, a **Cohesive Work Group,** requires minimal teamwork. At this level workers are in the same work group, but their work is independent. Level B, an **Efficient Work Team,** requires working as a self-directed team. At this level the team members' work is interdependent. Level C, an **Effective Organizational Unit,** requires shared teaming. At this level the team is interdependent with other organizational teams.

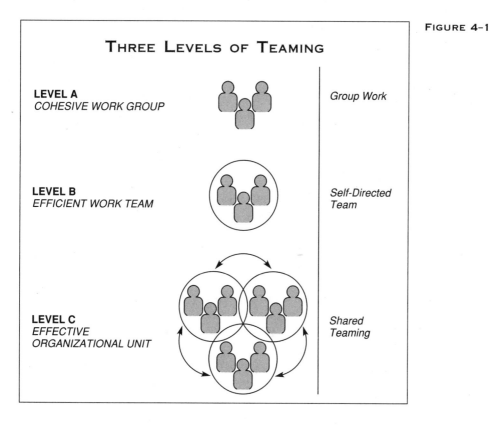

FIGURE 4–1

THREE LEVELS OF TEAMING

LEVEL A
COHESIVE WORK GROUP
Group Work

LEVEL B
EFFICIENT WORK TEAM
Self-Directed Team

LEVEL C
EFFECTIVE ORGANIZATIONAL UNIT
Shared Teaming

Group Work

LEVEL A: COHESIVE WORK GROUP

At Level A, a Cohesive Work Group, team members identify with one another as part of the same work group, but their work is primarily independent of one anothers'. Though they do not need to share work assignments with each other, the members are a "group" because the output of all the individuals comes from a single work unit.

- There is a shared purpose or goal(s).
- The individuals feel accepted by and able to influence one another.

  *A **Cohesive Work Group** focuses on the needs of its individual members.*

Self-Directed Team

LEVEL B: EFFICIENT WORK TEAM

At Level B, an Efficient Work Team, the team focuses on increasing its efficiency. Its members are interdependent—that is, they need the work of one another to achieve shared goals. As well as having the attributes of a cohesive work group, an efficient work team:

- Functions as an autonomous subunit within an organization.
- Has members who share task information with one another.
- Has a purpose, project, and goal(s) that are shared and understood by all members.

  *An **Efficient Work Team** focuses on increasing its efficiency in accomplishing work tasks as a self-directed team.*

Shared Teaming

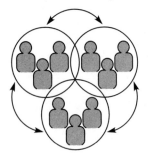

LEVEL C: EFFECTIVE ORGANIZATIONAL UNIT

At Level C, an Effective Organizational Unit, the focus is on the needs of the organization as a whole. The word *unit* is used to describe a team with a number of individuals and subteams having different assignments and performing various stages of the work. An Effective Organizational Unit incorporates the attributes of both a Cohesive Work Group and an Efficient Work Team, plus:

CHAPTER FOUR

- The team links with other organizational teams or functions for the completion of shared projects.

- The team's resources, both human and material, are shared with other organizational teams or functions.

- The team operates with a political and strategic perspective within the organization.

- Members flow in and out of the team according to the needs and timing of the project or ongoing work.

  *An **Effective Organizational Unit** integrates its work into the larger organization, works collaboratively with other teams, and functions in a manner of shared teaming.*

These introductory pages of the chapter and the *Three Levels of Teaming* checklist in Figure 4–2 provide basic information regarding the three levels for you and your co-team members to review and discuss. Use the checklist to consider the level or combination of levels at which your team is *currently* working and the level at which you perceive your team *should* be working. More specifics on how to work at levels A, B, and C, including WorkStyle trends for each level, are contained in the balance of this chapter.

How to Work at Level A

Group Work

A Cohesive Work Group

- Assumes responsibility for individual work within the context of a work group or function.
- Shares information for awareness of total group output.
- Allows for individual identity, creativity, and visibility.
- Develops congenial working relationships.
- Has group socials or gatherings to encourage a pleasant working environment.

Characteristics of Level A—Group Work

- Identification first with individual work and second with that of the group.
- Decision-making processes with individual and group input.

FIGURE 4-2

THREE LEVELS OF TEAMING: CHARACTERISTICS*†		
LEVEL A COHESIVE WORK GROUP *Group Work*	**LEVEL B** EFFICIENT WORK TEAM *Self-Directed Team*	**LEVEL C** EFFECTIVE ORGANIZATIONAL UNIT *Shared Teaming*
Most required characteristics of a cohesive work group:	*Most required characteristics of an efficient work team:*	*Most required characteristics of an effective organizational unit:*
❏ Identification first with individual work and second with that of the group.	❏ High identification with own team.	❏ More awareness of other teams; less "own team" identity.
❏ Decision-making processes with individual and group input.	❏ Decision-making process shared among team members.	❏ Decision-making process shared between teams and with other parts of the organization.
❏ Formal communication sessions for sharing of group results. Minimal requirement for informal or spontaneous communication.	❏ Extensive feedback and clarification within own team. Frequent informal or spontaneous communication.	❏ Extensive use of intra- and interteam feedback and clarification. Communication in "our organization" terms.
❏ Segregated assignments with minimal sharing of work tasks or integrating of work objectives.	❏ Common knowledge base among team members with work processes and production problems.	❏ Continuous checking of other teams' progress and realignment of the work.
❏ Comfortable group atmosphere.	❏ Unity and mutual support to defend team purpose and goals. "Our team" identity.	❏ General tone is collaborative for satisfaction of everyone in the organization, "betterment of the whole."
❏ Basic respect and mutual support for individuals' knowledge and skills.	❏ Mutual respect and admiration within team for accomplishment of shared goals.	❏ Conscious effort to build trust with other teams and other parts of the organization.
❏ Synergy from group recognition of individual contributions.	❏ Synergy from feelings of winning through accomplishment of "own team" goals.	❏ Synergy from feelings of winning through goal accomplishment for the total organization.

* This checklist is located in Appendix II: Checklists.

† Use this checklist to assess the level of teaming required.

- Formal communication sessions for sharing of group results. Minimal requirement for informal or spontaneous communication.

- Segregated assignments with minimal sharing of work tasks or integrating of work objectives.

- Comfortable group atmosphere.

- Basic respect and mutual trust for individual's knowledge and skills.

- Synergy from group recognition of individual contributions.

WORKSTYLE TRENDS—LEVEL A: GROUP WORK

Although the trend of working in teams is currently sweeping through organizations, a significant portion of the workforce may resist team participation. WorkStyle Patterns™ data show workforce discomfort with the teaming approach.

According to a WorkStyle Patterns™ study group of 9,311 employed individuals (primarily from North America), 23 percent like to work independently and manage their own work. These people want to work autonomously and neither coordinate the work of others nor have their work coordinated.

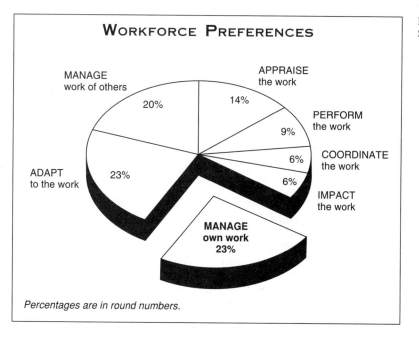

WORKFORCE PREFERENCES

MANAGE work of others — 20%
APPRAISE the work — 14%
PERFORM the work — 9%
COORDINATE the work — 6%
IMPACT the work — 6%
MANAGE own work — 23%
ADAPT to the work — 23%

Percentages are in round numbers.

McFletcher WorkStyle Patterns™ Study Group, 1995.

Individuals who prefer to work independently by managing their own work experience conflict between how they want to work and how the work must be done. These members of the workforce prefer Level A group work, which offers individual accountability, some degree of specialization, and minimal coordination. (See Appendix I: Resources for further information on the WorkStyle Patterns™ Normative Data Base.)

Self-Directed Team

How to Work at Level B

An Efficient Work Team:

- Assumes shared responsibility for planning as well as implementing.
- Paces and organizes the work so members can work both individually and with others as needed.
- Designs the work so that members depend upon each other's experience, abilities, and commitment in order to arrive at mutual goals.
- Assumes accountability as a self-directed team within a larger organizational context.
- Holds frequent meetings and information exchanges in group sessions.
- Shares information with co-team members to help with everyone's work.
- Shares facilities and equipment among own team members.
- Agrees upon the format for working together *before* planning such matters as:

  Physical layout of respective area(s).

  Goals.

  Agenda(s).

  Tasks.

  Each person's role.

  Working structure.

  Decision-making and problem solving methods, and so forth.
- Creates roles of group recorder and group facilitator to help the process or give feedback.

CHARACTERISTICS OF LEVEL B—SELF-DIRECTED TEAM

- High identification with own team.
- Decision-making processes shared among team members.
- Extensive feedback and clarification within own team. Frequent informal or spontaneous communication.
- Common knowledge base among team members with work processes and production problems.
- Unity and mutual support to defend team purpose and goals. "Our team" identity.
- Mutual respect and admiration within team for accomplishment of shared goals.
- Synergy from feelings of winning through accomplishment of own team goals.

WORKSTYLE TRENDS—LEVEL B: SELF-DIRECTED TEAM

The concept of self-directed work teams began with the assignment of the "whole job" to groups of individuals. This "whole job" concept (whether it meant the assembly of the *whole* car, janitorial service for the *whole* facility, or sales for the *whole* product line) established the need for groups of individuals who represented a mix of the required skills to complete the work together—as a team. These groups were formed as Level B self-directed teams.

WorkStyle Patterns™ data reveal common trends among teams that assume shared responsibility for planning and implementing the whole job. These trends vary somewhat according to industry and profession types. Manufacturing and service teams have similar work-approach requirements. Technical team work-approach trends are different from those of manufacturing and service teams but appear to be consistent across various industries in which work is highly technical.

Manufacturing and Service Teams

Manufacturing embarked upon the development of self-directed teams in the 1980s as a means to survive in a very competitive global industry. Team members learned about the "whole job" and developed multiple skills to perform all the work processes. This reduced the number of people required to do the work, decreased the product output time, reduced quality errors, and eliminated coverage problems when individuals were absent.

This same trend of instituting self-directed teams is now emerging in other industries and professions that require a competitive advantage; industries such as finance and health care, and professions such as customer service, human resources, and marketing. These industries and professions are experiencing a major shift from specialized roles with a professional identity to generalist roles. Examples include shifts such as compensation manager to human resource representative and registered nurse to health care facilitator.

Level B self-directed teams for the manufacturing and service industries require *adapting* and *coordinating* responsibilities; this includes a combination of coordination and task activities as well as a high level of responsiveness. Some organizations are relying on improved hiring and selection methods to seek out individuals who prefer to work this way (23 percent of the workforce studied prefer this WorkStyle). Organizations are also structuring their team environments to utilize other members of the workforce through a combination of generalist and specialist roles, and they are instituting systems and procedures to help meet coordination requirements.

Technical Teams

Team members from technically oriented teams, such as engineering design and development groups, are expected to work at a high level of competency as specialists while also linking their work to the work of others; they are to *perform* as instructed and *coordinate* as well. Individuals representing this segment of the workforce, however, prefer neither to coordinate the work nor merely perform the work but to manage their own work independently. (Compared with the norm of 23 percent for the general workforce, technically oriented members of the workforce prefer to work independently to a much higher degree. For example, of the accountants studied, 35 percent; electronic engineers, 43 percent; and neurologists, 46 percent.)

Members of self-directed technical teams are responsible for the success of the whole team as well their own. The reality, as evidenced from WorkStyle Patterns™ data, is that in technical team environments, regardless of the title the team holds or the expectations stated by the organization, there is only a moderate shift on the part of the team members from *performing* the work as individuals to also *coordinating* the work requirements.

If you are a member of a technically oriented team whose work processes are in the design or development stage, how might this information affect you and your team? A yes answer to any one of the following questions may indicate that you and/or your co-team members are working at Level A, group work, rather than at Level B, self-directed team.

- Due to a lack of sharing work processes or information, are you duplicating efforts or missing useful information that could save time and costs?

- Do other team members sometimes complain that you fail to involve them enough and, in turn, cause extra work or confusion for them, you, or your team?

- Are you concentrating so much on creating and controlling your own work processes that you and your co-team members are not learning from one another?

- Do you and your co-team members segregate the work processes into separate units of work with individual assignments? Should certain individuals be absent, would your team be in a difficult position due to dependency on those individuals' unique capabilities or knowledge?

How to Work at Level C

An Effective Organizational Unit:

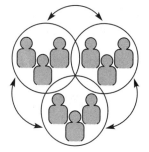

Shared Teaming

- Plans ways to discover and share team values with other groups.

- Establishes mutual trust in the organization through activities such as interteam planning, problem solving, and goal setting.

- Negotiates resolutions for production or organizational problems to establish boundaries and areas of compromise *before* the formal discussion or negotiations.

- Shares perceptions before and during problem-solving or negotiation sessions, especially where pressure can lead to a win–lose situation.

- Helps all individuals and teams succeed.
- Is open to more than just "own team" solutions in problem solving or negotiation.
- Finds ways to officially recognize other teams' successes.
- Clarifies work processes and production expectations with other teams and other parts of the organization.

CHARACTERISTICS OF LEVEL C—SHARED TEAMING

- More awareness of other teams; less "own team" identity.
- Decision-making processes shared between teams and with other parts of the organization.
- Extensive use of both intra and interteam feedback and clarification. Communication in "our organization" terms.
- Continuous checking of other teams' progress and realignment of the work.
- General tone is collaborative for satisfaction of everyone in the organization; "betterment of the whole."
- Conscious effort to build trust with other teams and other parts of the organization.
- Synergy from feelings of winning through goal accomplishment for the total organization.

WORKSTYLE TRENDS—LEVEL C: SHARED TEAMING

The days of the big corner office, clerical assistance, and individual assignments are rapidly disappearing. Today's workplace offers 4' × 5' cubicles, laptop computers, lots of teamwork and customer partnering. The net effect is a workplace where positions increasingly require flexibility and responsiveness.

This environment requires that individuals accept change quickly and recognize and react to new opportunities as they arise. This approach also requires that people seek out and maintain communication networks with all segments of the organization. They must appraise situations and alter work procedures quickly when problems arise. The WorkStyle approach of *adapting to the work* is characteristic of Level C—shared teaming.

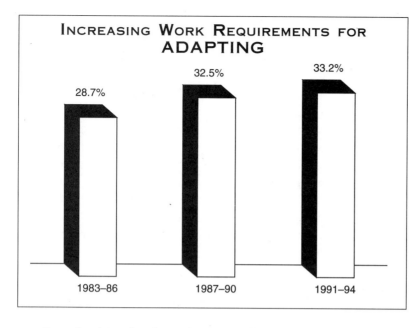

INCREASING WORK REQUIREMENTS FOR ADAPTING

28.7% — 1983–86
32.5% — 1987–90
33.2% — 1991–94

McFletcher WorkStyle Patterns™ Study Group, 1995.

Organizations that incorporate requirements to adapt at Level C teaming consider how work flows on a process basis rather than breaking it into incremental parts. These organizations are using a "whole systems" approach; involving their workforce in business decisions as well as work aspects, managing the progression of new technology and work processes, and teaming with customers for integrated responses.

It was mentioned earlier in the chapter that a sizable portion of the North American workforce from the WorkStyle Patterns™ study group (23 percent) report a preference for working in a responsive, adaptive mode. These people provide the flexibility needed to shift from doing the work to coordinating the work to managing the work. This same WorkStyle is required for Level B manufacturing and service self-directed teams. Being responsive to change, however, on a broader organizational basis rather than just within the team, is characteristic of Level C teaming; members flow in and out of teams according to the needs and timing of the project or ongoing work. (See the *Workforce Preferences* pie chart on page 39 and *Increasing Work Requirements for Adapting,* above.)

Consider carefully how much adapting, coordinating, and project management are truly required for your team. As organizations restructure for teams and participatory environments, people find themselves with new reporting structures, new work requirements, and new ways of coping. For effective teaming, it is imperative to clarify your team's reporting structure, work requirements, and behaviors.

Many organizations are developing a dual role concept for their team members: member-of-the-organization (generalist role) and member-of-a-team (specialist role). This dual role structure provides more avenues for using preferences of the workforce. Some people are more comfortable when performing their duties as a member of the organization and others when carrying out their specific team assignments.

In order to perform the generalist role, everyone in the organization receives the same training and information about the organization's goals, results, and customer requirements. Everyone also interfaces directly with customers and vendors and meets basic philosophical expectations in support of the organizational culture. This allows for more opportunities to utilize workforce preferences to "impact the work" and "manage own work."

For individuals performing the specialist role, assignments or positions are more clearly defined to both "perform" the work and "adapt" to the work. This corresponds with findings from the WorkStyle Patterns™ data base for self-directed teams.

Consider the best way to structure the assignments in your team to meet the needs of both the work and your team members' preferences. Give those who prefer to work more independently the more individualized assignments. Assign coordination activities to those who prefer group involvement and the project management accountabilities to those who enjoy forecasting, as well as coordinating, the work.

Team Situation

A Fortune 500 company, with U.S. Department of Defense (DoD) contracts for weapons design and manufacturing, bid for a new program that a competitor had held for several years. Odds of winning the contract were at best 40 percent, as there were many other challenges and conflicting concerns from the parent company, DoD, the U.S. Army, and the local community. Of particular concern was the issue of the local workforce, which had become accustomed to standardized pay and hours. How could a workforce with more of an entrepreneurial and organizational perspective be recruited?

A core team was assigned to draft the business development plan including a mission and guiding principles. The people on this core team felt honored and excited to have the chance to do something different for the U.S. business sector and the workforce in general. They created a "day in the life of the plant" simulation to determine how the organizational structure, work processes, and hiring and selection methods should be designed.

The new subsidiary was established to operate fairly autonomously with a flat organizational structure. The structure consisted of a general manager, five process teams, and a coordination group whose members also served as the process team leaders. The work was designed for Level B activities within the process teams; a Level C generalist role was designed for all members to serve as representatives of the total organization and to assure the process teams would also interface at Level C. The *Teams in Action* example (Figure 4–3) illustrates the teaming characteristics selected by the core team.

Team Process: Selection Process through Team Interviews

To meet its Level B and Level C teaming characteristics, this division created a three-role concept:

1. Generalist role for everyone as a member of the organization—*all-member-team-role.*
2. A generic *process team role* for each of the five process teams.
3. Specific *team member assignment roles.*

Teams in Action

FIGURE 4-3
TEAMS IN ACTION EXAMPLE

THREE LEVELS OF TEAMING—PROCESS TEAM SELECTIONS

LEVEL A COHESIVE WORK GROUP *Group Work*	LEVEL B EFFICIENT WORK TEAM *Self-Directed Team*	LEVEL C EFFECTIVE ORGANIZATION UNIT *Shared Teaming*
Most required characteristics of a cohesive work group:	*Most required characteristics of an efficient work team:*	*Most required characteristics of an effective Organizational unit:*
❑ Identification first with individual work and second with that of the group.	☑ High identification with own team.	☑ More awareness of other teams; less "own team" identity.
❑ Decision-making processes with individual and group input.	☑ Decision-making process shared among team members.	❑ Decision-making process shared between teams and with other parts of the organization.
❑ Formal communication sessions for sharing of group results. Minimal requirement for informal or spontaneous communication.	☑ Extensive feedback and clarification within own team. Frequent informal or spontaneous communication.	☑ Extensive use of intra- and interteam feedback and clarification. Communication in "our organization" terms.
❑ Segregated assignments with minimal sharing of work tasks or integrating work objectives.	☑ Common knowledge base among team members with work processes and production problems.	☑ Continuous checking of other teams' progress and realignment of the work.
☑ Comfortable group atmosphere.	❑ Unity and mutual support to defend team purpose and goals. "Our team" identity.	☑ General tone is collaborative for satisfaction of everyone in the organization, "betterment of the whole."
☑ Basic respect and mutual support for individuals' knowledge and skills.	☑ Mutual respect and admiration within team for accomplishment of shared goals.	☑ Conscious effort to build trust with other teams and other parts of the organization.
❑ Synergy from group recognition of individual contributions.	❑ Synergy from feelings of winning through accomplishment of "own team" goals.	❑ Synergy from feelings of winning through goal accomplishment for the total organization.

The subsidiary adopted a *team-based hiring and selection* plan for each of the three roles. Every member of the organization learned basic interviewing techniques in order to participate in the selection process when appropriate.

Human resource and staffing experts were consulted to create a compensation program to help attract the desired workforce and to address the labor cost aspect of the competitive bid. The new program included a skill-based team pay structure plus an incentive program at fiscal year-end according to cost savings. An incentive pool was incorporated to be divided among *all* employees.

Process Steps for Team-Based Hiring and Selection (to Assure Teaming at Levels B and C):

1. **Planning and work design for team assignment:**
   - Identify team members who will participate in the interviews and determine how these team members will interface with the team assignment.
   - Review assignment's purpose.
   - Conduct work design sessions to determine assignment activities.
   - Determine WorkStyle Profile for the assignment (see Appendix I: Resources for WorkStyle Patterns™ Inventory information).
   - Write description for each assignment.
   - Post, circulate, advertise.

2. **Interview preparation and practice:**
   - Plan team interview process and set timetable.
   - Have the interview team create interview questions for both phone prescreen and on-site team interview sessions.
   - Conduct practice interviews for each new assignment; include human resource consultation.
   - Evaluate practice and interview process and questions; revise if necessary. (See Figure 4–4 for an example of an interview question.)
   - Design ranking criteria sheets.

FIGURE 4-4
TEAMS IN ACTION EXAMPLE

TEAM-BASED HIRING AND SELECTION— INTERVIEW QUESTIONS

Preface—example:

"We are an organization that practices integrated product development and continuous improvement. The following questions are designed for us to learn about

- Your experience, knowledge, and skills.
- Your insights, thoughts, and general philosophy about the different subjects covered.

We will also present some typical scenarios to learn how you would apply the things you have learned."

Example of open-ended questions:

"Creating the right structure for both the product development and manufacturing stages of the product development cycle is important."

"Describe how you would go about establishing an inventory control program in a start-up situation."

"What type of systems would you put in place to provide a balance between product development and final manufacturing?"

Examples of direct probes:

- How do you define inventory control?
- How do you measure cycle time?
- How do you define capacity planning?
- How do you achieve high-speed performance in manufacturing?

3. Team interviews:

- Prepare candidates for interview process; explain how it will be different from typical one-on-one interview.
- Let candidates experience the work culture (tour, lunch, etc.).
- Conduct interviews.

4. Candidate screening and selection:

- Contact initial references.
- Review references and background information.
- Assess candidates and make selection via criteria established by the team; obtain consensus.

- Make offer.
- Write notification and appreciation letters to all candidates.
- Obtain feedback from candidates on process—both those selected and those not selected.

5. **WorkStyle assessment and team support:**
   - Develop performance and development plan for person selected.
   - Examine how each person prefers to work compared with the team assignment requirements (see Appendix I: Resources for WorkStyle Patterns™ Data Base.)
   - Assign support roles to team members to assure the person is well received, is well supported, and can succeed.

TEAM RESULTS

A WorkStyle Patterns™ study was completed with this group to determine the impact the three-role concept for approaching the work might have on the employees and the division.

The study compared each employee's preferred WorkStyle with the actual required WorkStyle of the following positions and assignments:

1. Their positions at other companies prior to joining this new subsidiary.
2. The generic process team role for each employee's assigned process team.
3. Their team member assignment with this new subsidiary.
4. The subsidiary's all-member role for the first year in startup.
5. The subsidiary's all-member role for the second year, as the work becomes more defined and progresses.

The WorkStyle Patterns™ study revealed that 53 percent of the initial employees hired for the new division had a preference for thinking organizationally—to help the division succeed. They wanted to do this by managing the work of others, appraising the work, or impacting the work through influencing goals and results. But when performing their team member assignments, many needed to tuck their preference aside and perform at a micro level to assure development and production work would be performed to perfection.

The study also revealed good and bad news. The good news was that the employees were quite comfortable with what was required in order to be a member of the division and to meet its overall goals. This comfort level was significantly more than that which they felt in their positions at previous places of employment.

The bad news is that the required approach for their daily routine work might cause stress due to preference for doing less specific tasks, through performing or managing own work, than their team assignments require.

McFletcher WorkStyle Patterns™
Study Group, 1995.

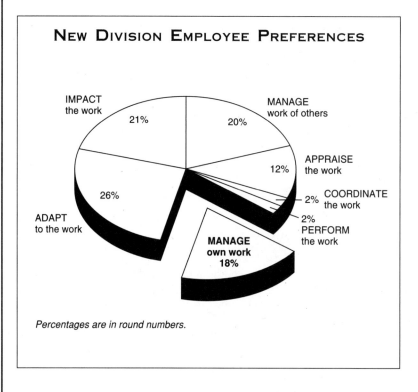

NEW DIVISION EMPLOYEE PREFERENCES

IMPACT the work 21%

MANAGE work of others 20%

APPRAISE the work 12%

COORDINATE the work 2%

PERFORM the work 2%

MANAGE own work 18%

ADAPT to the work 26%

Percentages are in round numbers.

The hiring process had mixed results. The team-based hiring and selection steps were not always followed. There was an immense workload for the few who were on the initial core team. Sometimes they bypassed the ideal model of designing the work, creating the questions, and facilitating team interviews. Instead, individual team leaders would hire individually, which seemed quicker and more efficient. When this happened it caused resentment and feelings of self-righteousness among those who were "following the principles." Without fail, those hired in the traditional way did not understand nor commit to the team culture as easily. This caused confusion and misunderstandings.

In most cases, however, the team selection process was followed. It generated an inspired, committed, hardworking group of employees.

The division's first-year production results were astounding and were the "pride and joy" of the Department of Defense. Product rollout occurred two months ahead of schedule with $15 million cost savings. The employees were rewarded from the cost savings through the "all" team member incentive program.

CHAPTER FIVE

Understanding Team Support Roles

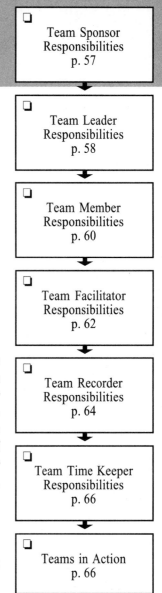

❑ Team Sponsor Responsibilities p. 57

❑ Team Leader Responsibilities p. 58

❑ Team Member Responsibilities p. 60

❑ Team Facilitator Responsibilities p. 62

❑ Team Recorder Responsibilities p. 64

❑ Team Time Keeper Responsibilities p. 66

❑ Teams in Action p. 66

The Teams in Action *story in this chapter exemplifies a typical "high-tech," "low-touch" engineering design group. The design members of this group perceived no need to team their design projects, particularly with test technicians, product developers, or their managers. The* Team Member Checklist *in this chapter was used for an exercise during a team session to help all the team members understand their accountabilities to one another as well as to other individuals and teams within the organization. This same exercise may be helpful for your team.*

• • •

There are six key support roles that help a team function effectively:

- Team sponsor
- Team leader
- Team member
- Team facilitator
- Team recorder
- Team time keeper

In groups with over 15 members, each role can be assigned to a different person. In smaller groups, however, these roles are usually combined, such as leader/facilitator, or facilitator/recorder, or facilitator/recorder/time keeper. Members filling these roles may or may not rotate during the life of a team.

Using a facilitator from outside the team is an option if the team leader or one or more of the team members cannot or should not function as a facilitator at team meetings. There are a variety of reasons for having external assistance, such as complexity of the agenda, issues among team members, need for objectivity, or a lack of facilitation skills among the team members. It is suggested that teams use a skilled external or internal facilitator to get their team started, identify team goals, and model facilitation techniques.

Throughout this chapter there are sample checklists for each support role (Figures 5–1 through 5–4), summarizing the role's responsibilities. The checklists can be used as a reminder, a self-assessment tool, or a team-building experience. The *Teams in Action* section at the end of this chapter illustrates how to maximize the use of these checklists.

Team Sponsor

The **team sponsor** assumes ownership and accountability for a team's assignment and serves as a mentor to the team. The sponsor is the link to the rest of the organization, keeps others informed of the team's progress, and runs interference for the team.

Team Leader

The **team leader** keeps the team focused on its task and works closely with the team sponsor to link the team to the larger organization.

Team Members

Team members collaborate with one another and the leader to set and achieve the team's goals, to work together as a team, and to present recommendations.

Team Facilitator (optional)

The **team facilitator** ensures that team members participate in decision making as equals. The facilitator guides the team into recommendations made by consensus, rather than by one or more dominant members.

Team Recorder

The **team recorder** carries the responsibility of capturing, on paper, the ideas and decisions of the group at the team meetings.

Team Time Keeper

The **team time keeper** makes sure the agenda has allotted times for each item and informs the team of time allowances and constraints.

TEAM SPONSOR RESPONSIBILITIES

ROLE

To mentor the team while assuming ownership and accountability for the team's assignment. The sponsor is usually a manager who has direct responsibility or familiarity with the work of the team. The sponsor does not manage or control either the team or the work of the team, but serves in an advisory and supportive capacity.

TASKS

- Define the boundaries of the team's work with input from the related functions.
- Select a team leader.
- Keep leadership informed of team progress.
- Run interference when the team experiences blockages, priority difficulties, conflicts, interteam conflicts, or schedule problems.
- Receive and review team reports.
- Outside own area of accountability, assist with integrating the team implementation, implement recommendations and funding within own area of accountability.
- Visit and observe team meetings periodically to address concerns and stimulate motivation.

- Keep informed about other teams' activities and look for opportunities to integrate with own team's work. Share this information with the team leader.

- Review and critique recommendations.

TEAM LEADER RESPONSIBILITIES

ROLE

To keep the team focused on its task and to provide the key link between the team and other parts of the organization.

TASKS

- Help the team clarify its goals.
- Clarify organizational expectations and constraints.
- Help the team achieve a sense of oneness and trust.
- Influence team members to cooperate, resolve conflict, communicate openly, and contribute to the team's task.
- Keep the team on track and performing.
- Help team members get needed resources and data.
- Act as a project manager to ensure the agenda is covered and action items are completed.
- Help team members understand their roles.
- Solicit team member and facilitator input on agenda items.
- Prepare and distribute team meeting agenda.
- Bring in a team facilitator as needed to help the team progress toward its goal.
- Work with the team facilitator and team recorder to ensure successful team meetings.
- Provide information and opinions without dominating the team.
- Ensure balanced participation and input from all team members.
- Guide the group in using a consensus-type approach to decision making.
- Allow self to be influenced by team members. Ask for feedback on the team results as well as on your performance.

See *Role Checklist for the Team Leader* (Figure 5–1).

FIGURE 5-1

ROLE CHECKLIST FOR THE TEAM LEADER*†

Please answer the following questions by placing a check (✔) in the appropriate column.

The Team Leader	Does Not Do	Does Sometimes	Does Consistently
1. Helps the group focus and maintain its energy toward the task by:			
• Soliciting team member input on agenda items prior to meetings.	❏	❏	❏
• Preparing and distributing agenda at least two days before meetings.	❏	❏	❏
• Working with the facilitator to ensure the meeting space is free of distractions.	❏	❏	❏
• Arranging meeting room furniture to maximize communication.	❏	❏	❏
• Keeping the group on track during the meeting.	❏	❏	❏
2. Helps keep the facilitator and recorder in their respective roles by:			
• Discussing the agenda, goals and issues prior to meetings.	❏	❏	❏
• Calling upon both to perform their functions during meetings.	❏	❏	❏
3. Initiates in setting directions for the group.	❏	❏	❏
4. Clarifies organizational expectations and constraints.	❏	❏	❏
5. Provides information and opinions based upon technical knowledge but does not dominate group.	❏	❏	❏
6. Guides the group in terms of its decision making, seeking consensus-type approach.	❏	❏	❏
7. Evaluates group's progress in relation to task and gives feedback to all members.	❏	❏	❏
8. Represents the group in the larger organization.	❏	❏	❏

Adapted from *How to Make Meetings Work*, Doyle and Strauss, 1976, Wyden Books.

* This checklist is located in Appendix II: Checklists.

† Use this checklist to discuss team leader effectiveness.

TEAM MEMBER RESPONSIBILITIES

ROLE

To be accountable for the quality of the team's decisions. To collaborate with other team members to successfully achieve the team's goals.

TASKS

Each member is expected to attend meetings and to contribute his or her expertise and creativity fully so that the team is productive.

- Participate in setting team goals.
- Offer information, knowledge, and expertise to help the team achieve its goals.
- Attend and fully participate in team meetings.
- Participate in a consensus-type approach to decision making (seek solutions that satisfy the whole team).
- Support the team leader in his or her leadership role.
- Complete agreed-upon action items.
- Support the team's decisions.
- Be willing to sacrifice for the good of the team.
- Listen actively to other team members and strive to understand others' viewpoints.
- Avoid excessive pleading of own causes and concerns.
- Give credit to other team members.
- Support organizational expectations and constraints.
- Help the team resolve interpersonal issues that may have a negative impact on the team's performance.
- Assist the team leader in keeping the team on track and performing.
- Help other team members get the resources and data they need.
- Offer input on agenda items for team meetings.
- Provide information and opinions without dominating the team.
- Assure your thoughts are understood and also captured accurately in the team notes.

See *Role Checklist for Team Members* (Figure 5–2).

FIGURE 5-2

ROLE CHECKLIST FOR THE TEAM MEMBER*†

Please answer the following questions by placing a check (✔) in the appropriate column.

The Team Member:

	Does Not Do	Does Sometimes	Does Consistently
1. Helps the team focus and maintain energy toward the task by:			
• Supporting the team's charter and mission.	❑	❑	❑
• Being present and attentive at team meetings.	❑	❑	❑
• Asking questions and seeking clarity regarding the task.	❑	❑	❑
• Avoiding getting stuck on own opinion or solution.	❑	❑	❑
2. Participates in all aspects of the team's work by:			
• Listening to others.	❑	❑	❑
• Offering own ideas and suggestions.	❑	❑	❑
• Volunteering to take appropriate action items.	❑	❑	❑
• Keeping others posted and informed.	❑	❑	❑
3. Supports team cohesiveness by:			
• Drawing out ideas and participation from other team members.	❑	❑	❑
• Communicating own needs, concerns, and feelings.	❑	❑	❑
• Validating other team members' needs, concerns, and feelings.	❑	❑	❑
• Helping others achieve their action items.	❑	❑	❑
• Asking for help when needed.	❑	❑	❑
4. Supports synergy and creativity by:			
• Learning creative tools and participating in creative team sessions.	❑	❑	❑
• Exploring alternatives for all decisions.	❑	❑	❑

Adapted from *How to Make Meetings Work,*
Doyle and Strauss, 1976, Wyden Books.

* This checklist is located in Appendix II: Checklists.

† Use this checklist to discuss team member effectiveness.

TEAM FACILITATOR RESPONSIBILITIES

ROLE

To ensure that team members participate as equals and that recommendations are made by consensus, not by the opinions of a dominant member or one of superior influence.

The team facilitator is often someone outside the team who has training and experience in group process and whose primary contribution to the team is to facilitate the team process. Experienced team members may choose to rotate this role when a team is fully functioning and self-monitoring.

TASKS

- Conduct team meetings.
- Remain neutral with regard to opinions and ideas about the team's tasks by returning questions of that nature to team members.
- Focus the energy of the group on a common task.
- Suggest appropriate methods and procedures for accomplishing the team's tasks.
- Protect individuals and their ideas from attack.
- Ensure that team members listen actively to one another and hear one another out without interrupting.
- Use processes and methods that encourage everyone to participate and gain influence in the group.
- Help the group clarify both its tasks and its guidelines (norms) for working together.
- Support and coach the recorder.
- Coach the team leader in group process.
- Clarify organizational expectations and constraints.
- Coordinate documentation of team sessions.
- Give feedback and evaluation of team progress.
- Work with the team leader to coordinate pre- and postmeeting logistics.

See Figure 5–3, *Role Checklist for Team Facilitator.*

FIGURE 5-3

ROLE CHECKLIST FOR THE TEAM FACILITATOR*†

Please answer the following questions by placing a check (✔) in the appropriate column.

The Team Facilitator:

	Does Not Do	Does Sometimes	Does Consistently
1. Helps each member of the team to fully participate by:			
• Gaining membership in the team.	❏	❏	❏
• Developing influence in the team.	❏	❏	❏
• Understanding the precise nature of the team's task assignment.	❏	❏	❏
• Developing a set of team operating norms that encourage individual participation.	❏	❏	❏
2. Makes observations and suggestions regarding the team's methods and procedures.	❏	❏	❏
3. Stays neutral with regard to opinions and ideas about the team's task by returning questions of that nature to team members.	❏	❏	❏
4. Protects members and their ideas from attack.	❏	❏	❏
5. Acts as a model for team members of how to be a productive member.	❏	❏	❏
6. Gives feedback to entire team and individual members as to how they are doing in their process.	❏	❏	❏
7. Gives support to the team recorder.	❏	❏	❏
8. Evaluates and provides feedback to team with regard to its development as a team.	❏	❏	❏
9. Helps with coordination of team's relations to outside elements.	❏	❏	❏
10. Coordinates pre- and postmeeting logistics.	❏	❏	❏

Adapted from *How to Make Meetings Work,*
Doyle and Strauss, 1976, Wyden Books

* This checklist is located in Appendix II: Checklists.
† Use this checklist to discuss team facilitator effectiveness.

TEAM RECORDER RESPONSIBILITIES

ROLE

To capture the ideas and decisions of the team and post in full view of the group.

The recorder can be a team member or someone from outside the team. When a team member serves as the recorder, it is important for him or her to remain neutral while recording. Some teams find it helpful to rotate the role of the recorder. The recorder takes notes on flip chart paper, with an overhead projector or by computer projection. All team members can see the ideas and decisions during the meeting. These should later be transcribed and copies circulated to the team before the next meeting.

TASKS

- Record enough of the speaker's ideas to be understood later; use key words.
- Avoid overediting or rewording what the speaker said.
- Remain neutral. (Do not contribute own ideas when recording.)
- Give the recording role to someone else when contributing own ideas.
- Stop the team when lagging behind; ask people to repeat or slow down.
- Make corrections when asked.
- When using flip charts, write legibly in letters large enough for everyone to see.
- Do not worry about spelling. (A spell checker software program can be used later.)
- Abbreviate words to keep up with the conversation.
- Use colors and symbols to highlight and/or divide ideas.
- Number and date all sheets.
- Avoid taking over for the facilitator or the team leader.
- Accept advice and direction from the facilitator or the team leader.
- Ensure the notes are typed or documented for team records.

See Figure 5–4, *Role Checklist for Team Recorder.*

FIGURE 5-4

ROLE CHECKLIST FOR THE TEAM RECORDER*†

Please answer the following questions by placing a check (✔) in the appropriate column.

The Team Recorder:

	Does Not Do	Does Sometimes	Does Consistently
1. Captures basic ideas on large sheets of paper in full view of the team:			
• Refrains from editing or paraphrasing.	❏	❏	❏
• Uses the words of the member speaking.	❏	❏	❏
• Records enough of the speaker's ideas so they can be understood later.	❏	❏	❏
2. Remains neutral by:			
• Refraining from contributing own ideas.	❏	❏	❏
• Keeping pace with the team. (If the recorder gets lost or does not hear, that is OK. He or she may stop the team and ask people to repeat or slow down.)	❏	❏	❏
• Supporting and following the facilitator.	❏	❏	❏
• Listening for key words versus writing every word.	❏	❏	❏
• Making corrections nondefensively.	❏	❏	❏
3. Provides a visual team memory by:			
• Printing/writing legibly with letters about an inch and a half high.	❏	❏	❏
• Writing fast.	❏	❏	❏
• Concerning self with content; not afraid of misspelling.	❏	❏	❏
• Abbreviating words to keep up with conversation.	❏	❏	❏
• Varying colors; using colors to highlight, divide ideas, underline.	❏	❏	❏
• Varying the size of writing/printing.	❏	❏	❏
• Using outline form.	❏	❏	❏
• Using stars, arrows, numbers, dots, and so forth.	❏	❏	❏
• Numbering all sheets.	❏	❏	❏

Adapted from *How to Make Meetings Work*, Doyle and Strauss, 1976, Wyden Books.

* This checklist is located in Appendix II: Checklists.

† Use this checklist to discuss team recorder effectiveness.

TEAM TIME KEEPER RESPONSIBILITIES

ROLE

To make sure the agenda has allotted times and to inform the team of time allowances and constraints.

TASKS

- Help the team allot adequate time for each agenda item.
- Appraise the team periodically of the time in relation to the allotted time.
- Gain knowledge of how long certain types of agenda items take; advise the team as it plans the agenda.
- Ensure team starts and ends on time—including breaks—no excuses!

TEAMS IN ACTION

TEAM SITUATION

A high-performance team in a prestigious engineering product design group was experiencing conflict when working together in meetings. They perceived that they got along quite well between meetings and were effective in their individual work. Their manager, on the other hand, was witnessing duplication in their work, designs that weren't well tested before going into development, some schedule slippage, and a lack of communication with customers. He began to hold regularly scheduled meetings to get the design engineers to communicate more consistently with the test technicians and product development engineers. He also hoped that more frequent and regularly scheduled meetings would diminish the confusion and conflict that occurred during the meetings. The members, however, accused their manager of lacking focus and sufficient reason for holding team meetings.

The manager brought in a facilitator to assist with team meetings. During team meetings the members soon shifted the blame for ineffective team sessions to the facilitator. The team members thought the team-building attempts instituted by the manager and facilitator were "touchy-feely" rather than a productive use of the team's time. They challenged the relevance of shared discussions in regard to each other's work projects because they did not think the discussion would benefit their individual design, test, and development assignments.

TEAM PROCESS

The facilitator and manager decided to confront the team with their lack of group member accountability and their unproductive norms such as challenging or withdrawing, rather than contributing, when someone else's ideas or assignments were being discussed. They used the team member checklist seen in Figure 5–5 and used the following process steps to work through the confrontation process. Figure 5–5 illustrates the team's results.

Process Steps:

1. Each team member completes the team member checklist.
2. Each team member states his or her responses to item 1 of the checklist. After item 1 is complete, continue with item 2; then repeat the process for items 3 and 4.
3. Record and tally the responses on an enlarged copy of the checklist.
4. Discuss the differences and similarities of the members' responses.
5. Continue the process until all four categories are recorded and discussed.
6. Identify team member activities that need to be performed more consistently.
7. Identify and prioritize which of these activities need to be addressed with a team plan.
8. Plan a strategy for how the team will carry out each of the prioritized activities.

TEAM RESULTS

The tallied results made it quite obvious that the group saw no reason to be a team. The manager used the results to share his concerns and frustrations with their individualistic mentality. He acknowledged that they each did quality, creative work as individual contributors, but not collectively. The team members admitted that they had no understanding of the need to work together and no appreciation for working as a team.

FIGURE 5-5
TEAMS IN ACTION EXAMPLE

TEAM MEMBER'S ACCOUNTABILITY

Role Checklist for the Team Member

November 12, 1994
Design Team X

Please review the following guidelines by placing a check (✔) in the appropriate column.

The Team Member:

	Does Not Do	Does Sometimes	Does Consistently
1. Helps the team focus and maintain energy toward the task by:			
Our Priorities ① Supporting the team's charter and mission.	☒ ⟍⟋⟍	❑ //	❑ /
Being present and attentive at team meetings.	❑ //	☒ ////	❑ /
Asking questions and seeking clarity on the task.	☒ ///	☒ ////	❑
Avoiding getting stuck on own opinion or solution.	❑ /	☒ ////	❑ //
2. Participates in all aspects of the team's work by:			
⑥ Listening to others.	❑ /	☒ ⟍⟋⟍	❑ /
③ Offering own ideas and suggestions.	☒ ⟍⟋⟍ /	❑ /	❑
④ Volunteering to take on appropriate action items.	☒ ⟍⟋⟍ //	❑	❑
Keeping others posted and informed.	☒ ////	❑ //	❑ /
3. Supports team cohesiveness by:			
⑤ Drawing out ideas and participation from other team members.	☒ ⟍⟋⟍	❑ /	❑ /
Communicating own needs, concerns, and feelings.	☒ ⟍⟋⟍	☒ //	❑
Validating other team members' needs, concerns, and feelings.	☒ ⟍⟋⟍ /	☒ /	❑
Helping others achieve their action items.	❑	☒ ////	❑ ///
Asking for help when needed.	❑ //	☒ ⟍⟋⟍	❑
4. Supports synergy and creativity by:			
② Learning creative tools and participating in creative team sessions.	☒ ////	☒ ///	❑
Exploring alternatives for all decisions.	☒ ////	☒ //	❑ /

Adapted from *How to Make Meetings Work*, Doyle and Strauss, 1976, Wyden Books.

The team members brainstormed and recorded the reasons and ways that they needed to work together. This was done to determine how much of their work should be autonomous and how much should be shared. To perform priority item 1, "supporting the team's charter and mission," they created their team mission and agreed upon future meeting times and methods for working together.

The manager assumed a combination role of team facilitator and team leader and has helped the team reach high levels of creativity while also reducing design costs. For the sake of the product introduction and roll-out goals, the team members accepted responsibility for the team member role. Though some members participated with reluctance, their participation was an improvement from their prior resistance. Improved coordination now exists between the test and development groups and with the customers.

CHAPTER SIX

WORKING TOGETHER

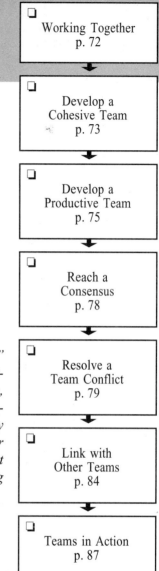

he Teams in Action *example for "Working Together" centers around a cross-functional team for an open systems software development project. Members of the team included planners, product marketers, software developers, schedulers, and documentation personnel. These people did not want to be teamed! They were concerned that teaming would complicate their work rather than increase efficiency. To discover ways they were and were not supportive of one another's work, they used the three team-building exercises presented in this chapter:*

- *The Six Elements of Healthy Teamwork.*
- *Team Development Cycle—Magic Circle.*
- *Conflict Resolution.*

Process steps and illustrations for you and your co-team members to use are included with their team story.

• • •

WORKING TOGETHER

There are three important dimensions of teamwork that have an impact on a team's performance:

- Cohesiveness, for developing sound relationships among the team's members.
- Productivity, for getting the work done.
- Integration, for linking with other teams.

An effective team continuously works in these three dimensions as illustrated below.

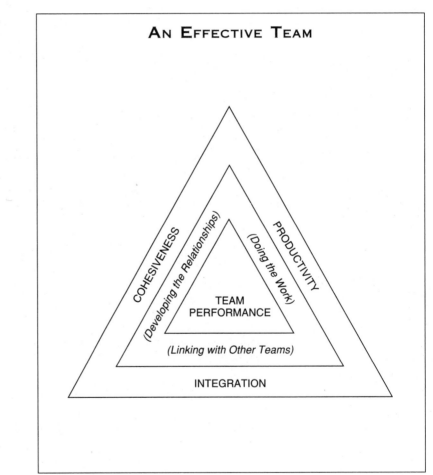

DEVELOP A COHESIVE TEAM

SIX ELEMENTS FOR HEALTHY TEAM RELATIONSHIPS[1]

For a team to experience cohesiveness, enjoy working together, and have a comfortable flow of the work, healthy relationships need to exist among team members. There are six elements for healthy team relationships.

1. MUTUAL TRUST

Of the six elements, mutual trust is the most significant and the most basic. When people trust each other, they can exercise freedom in their relationships. They can risk exposing their ideas, their feelings, and their concerns with the assurance that they won't be corrected, disputed, belittled, punished, or subtly put down. People need acceptance to feel secure with one another.

> *On a healthy team, team members feel secure and express their ideas, thoughts, feelings, and concerns.*

2. MUTUAL CONCERN

This is the quality of "otherness"—of having awareness of the feelings and needs of others and being willing and able to attend to those needs. People can risk being different and express their differences. When a group's attitude is one of mutual concern, "we-ness" is valued above "I-ness." There is a win–win kind of relationship that helps the whole group achieve, rather than just one person getting his or her way.

> *On a healthy team, team members can depend on one another to ensure that the whole comes out right. There is a spirit of collaboration.*

3. MUTUAL SUPPORT

Mutual support is trust and care in action. This manifests itself in the way members of the group help each other when they see one another in difficulty. It is the willingness of team members to help

---

one another out, to be observant enough to know when to come to each other's aid when there is a need for support.

> *On a healthy team, members take action to help and support one another. When one member is in difficulty, the others pitch in to help out.*

Note: *The above three ingredients—mutual trust, mutual concern, and mutual support—are much like the chicken and the egg. No one can really tell which comes first—which is the beginning and which the result. They are mutually reactive and supportive; they all feed each other; they are synergistic. If a team can get one ingredient started and working, the others tend to follow.*

4. GENERAL EMOTIONAL STATUS OF MEMBERS

This component of teamwork is very important and perhaps the most difficult to do anything about. When individual members feel negative emotionally due to things that are happening or have happened to them both in the organization and outside, it impacts the team. Such emotions can be a critical blockage to the achievement of the team's goals. Understanding and open communication among team members help to disclose and alleviate some of these feelings. Whenever possible, such emotions should be caringly addressed with honesty and fortitude by the other members.

> *On a healthy team, negative emotional concerns are diffused through the interested, caring attention of team members to one another. Individuals take responsibility for disclosure and sharing of their uncertainties, fears, and needs.*

5. MUTUAL RESPECT

In order for people who work together to develop the positive qualities that are discussed above, they must respect each other both as colleagues and as human beings. It is important for each team member to do the task well (as near perfection as humanly possible), do one's own part in getting common tasks done, and be positive, responsive and courteous to questions and suggestions of fellow workers.

> *Each person must conduct him- or herself as a professional at all times.*

6. MUTUAL CELEBRATION

Work, like life, can be serious and unforgiving. Each person must give his or her very best to help the whole to win—to succeed. There will be occasions when, in order for the team to win, an individual or two may become stars and the others will play only supporting roles. When this happens and when the team successfully reaches a goal on time and with high quality, it is time for a celebration. Celebrations should be built into the team's norms and values as recognition of the whole. The stars should, of course, be recognized, but no more than the supporting cast who helped them.

> *When good things happen, the entire team should take time out to celebrate.*

DEVELOP A PRODUCTIVE TEAM

HOW A TEAM DEVELOPS

When people gather together in teams, their concerns, interests, and work activities follow a predictable cycle. Understanding and meeting those needs in a systematic way can help teams become more effective.

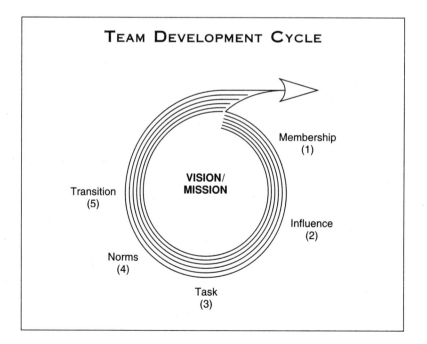

TEAM DEVELOPMENT CYCLE

VISION/MISSION

Membership (1)

Influence (2)

Task (3)

Norms (4)

Transition (5)

1. Membership

The first need people have is to feel accepted. They want to know on what basis they are a member of this team. They need to know that they are valued, not penalized, for their uniqueness and that diversity is an important element in teamwork.

Gaining acceptance and knowing one's place in the team are essential to constructively participating in the team's activities. Not being assured of the team's acceptance can lead members to act in ways that will impede the team's progress toward achievement.

Take time early on to learn about one another so that each member can be recognized and utilized. Discuss membership topics such as:

- Past work experiences—most enjoyed and least enjoyed.
- Prior or current team experiences—what was beneficial and what not.
- Understanding of the team assignment or purpose.
- Hopes for the outcomes of this team; what each member would like to contribute.

2. Influence

The second need team members have is to know how they can gain influence. This may be expressed in a number of ways, but the basic motivation is, How do I know people will listen to me?

Not being sure of one's degree of influence can lead members to act in ways that may hinder the meeting of the team's goals. Use each person's preferred WorkStyle as a way to discuss how he or she might best influence the group—some through their own expertise, some by adapting to the needs of the others, some by clarifying goals and results. Discuss how these experiences and skills will be utilized or brought to the team.

3. Task

Only when people have been assured of their acceptance and believe they will be listened to will they be ready to fully participate in the team's tasks or work activities. **Team tasks** or activities include actions that need to be performed to meet the team's goals and objectives.

Of course, to participate productively, people need to be clear about their tasks, be organized within the team, and have methods in place to receive and provide feedback. The team as a whole needs to have the commensurate authority and role clarity within its larger sphere of operation (within an organization, community, or nation) to be able to carry out its tasks.

When assigning tasks among team members, consider individual WorkStyle preferences as well as knowledge and skills. Different ways of both thinking about and doing the work aid a team in becoming more balanced. This addresses the second and third steps of the Team Model (Figure 3–2) illustrated earlier in Chapter 3, "Organizing the Team,"—aligning team members' preferences with team assignments. Suggestions for ways to address preferences are provided in that chapter as well.

4. Norms/Guidelines

As the members begin doing the team's tasks, they also begin the process of establishing practices that quickly become "the way we do things here." Over time, these practices become norms or unspoken group guidelines that govern a wide range of team and individual activities, from the manner in which team members interact with one another to how they perceive the outside world.

When norms or group guidelines are not routinely reviewed and questioned by the team they can become a hindrance to team performance. (See Chapter 3, "Organizing Teams," for a discussion on establishing team guidelines.)

5. Transition

Once the team tasks have been identified and completed, the work of the team transitions to a new phase. The new phase may include a second stage of sequential activities, a higher level of work, or a new project entirely. When this transition takes place, the team actually reenters the *Team Development Cycle* (see diagram on page 75) often without realizing it. Membership, influence, team tasks, and group norms may change and need to be revisited.

For many, leaving a team can be an emotional time. Healthy teams that either are disbanding or have members cycle in and out create ceremonies through which the team experience is crystalized for the individual. This allows the individual to carry positive experiences to his or her next team.

At some stage, everyone leaves their team. Much of what people learn in a team is carried forward to the next team experience.

SUMMARY

When teams or individuals are not performing well, it is helpful to review the five stages of needs in the team development cycle to determine if the root cause might be traced back to one of them.

REACH CONSENSUS

Team members are frequently confused about the concept of consensus. Some mistakenly think it means everyone must end up agreeing with everyone else. These members may be understandably apprehensive about being expected to achieve consensus, especially on topics and issues of long-standing concern and disagreement.

Here are some things to remember about consensus:

- Consensus does not mean 100 percent agreement. Consensus occurs when everyone can support a team decision 100 percent. It is a win–win solution in which everyone feels that a comfortable compromise has been reached and that no one feels they had to give in on any strongly held convictions or needs.
- Reaching consensus takes time. It often means finding a new solution that no one has thought of before, one that will serve everyone's strongest needs.
- Because consensus consumes time and energy, it should be reserved for important decisions that require a high degree of support from those who will implement them.

- Less important decisions can be delegated to a subgroup, to an individual team member, or to the team leader. **Caution:** *Make sure team members are not absolving themselves of responsibility or difficulty by simply letting someone else make the decision. Team members must fully support the decisions they delegate to someone else.*

RESOLVE TEAM CONFLICT

Team conflict falls into two categories:

1. A **core** or **central conflict**—one that impedes the team's progress toward its task completion or goal.

2. A **peripheral conflict**—one that exists but does not significantly hinder the team's progress toward its goal.

Core or central conflicts should be dealt with as constructively as possible. They should be surfaced, explored, understood, and considered so the team can come to a mutually agreeable solution.

Peripheral conflicts can be dealt with quickly during a team meeting. Outside the team's meetings, they can be tabled or ignored. The team as a whole should decide if a conflict is core or peripheral and agree on how to resolve it.

The four charts listed below and illustrated in Figures 6–1 through 6–4, provide tips for understanding and resolving conflict. The Teams in Action example tells how members of a team used one of the charts to identify the types of conflict they are most likely to experience.

- A Model for Conflict Utilization.

- Personal Choices in Dealing with Conflict.

- What Team Members Can Do to Help Resolve Conflict.

- What Team Leaders and Facilitators Can Do to Help Teams Resolve Conflict.

FIGURE 6-1

A MODEL FOR CONFLICT UTILIZATION

- Accept the conflict.

- Involve all parties to the conflict in the pursuit of the solution. This will:

    Give access to data on what the real conflict is.

    Assure ownership and shared understanding.

- Share perspectives, feelings, and opinions about the conflict/issue at hand.

- Share the facts and gather information. Sort facts from feelings and opinions.

    Get those involved to agree on the data needed.

    Involve everyone in the data gathering.

- Determine the level of conflict in order, from low to high:

    Information — Clarify the facts.

    Methods — Review or determine appropriate methods.

    Goals — Establish shared goals.

    Values — Use to heighten awareness only by sanctioning the worth of all beliefs and values.

- Identify desired outcomes by all parties involved.

- Develop a plan to come to a win–win solution.

Adapted from Conflict Model, Association of Personal and Organizational Development, 1975.

FIGURE 6-2

PERSONAL CHOICES IN DEALING WITH CONFLICT

When faced with a conflict situation, each of us has a choice about how to deal with the conflict. We can do any one of the following:

- *Withdraw* and avoid confronting the conflict altogether. You take whatever you can get, and you may lose.

- *Accommodate* the other person and give in to him or her. You let the other person win.

- *Compromise* by splitting the difference or trading (I'll do that for you as you do this for me). You both win a little and lose a little.

- *Defeat* the other person by getting your way through power, intimidation, negotiation, or other means. You win; the other person loses.

- *Collaborate* with the other person to creatively problem solve so both parties' needs are met. You and the other person create a new solution. You both win.

For important team conflicts, using the collaborative choice will help the team come to consensus and gain members' support in carrying out the decision. There are times, however, when each of the other choices may be appropriate, depending on the situation. Being aware of these choices and understanding the consequences of each helps team members deal more constructively with conflict.

Adapted from the Kenneth Thomas model of handling conflict behavior. M. Dunnette, ed., "Conflict and Conflict Management," in *Handbook of Industrial and Organizational Psychology,* (Chicago: Rand McNally, 1976).

FIGURE 6-3

WHAT TEAM MEMBERS CAN DO TO HELP TEAMS RESOLVE CONFLICT

- Keep the end goal in mind. Help others do the same.

- Actively consider others' views by:

    Listening.

    Finding merit in the other person's viewpoint.

    Understanding what the other person means (what are his or her main points?).

    Stating the other person's viewpoint back to them (to show you understand).

    Restating if you did not understand the first time or two.

    Avoiding defense of your own view until you have fully understood the other person's view.

- Don't hold back when you disagree or have another idea.

- State your own view clearly, firmly, and without excessive emotion.

- When interrupted, ask people to let you finish making your points.

- Once you have been heard, avoid harping on your own position. Let your idea stand on its own merit.

- Try not to get personally attached to or invested in your own position. Keep the end goal in mind. Don't take it personally if the team decides to take another approach.

- Offer suggestions instead of disagreeing with or criticizing someone else's approach.

- View team conflict as natural and help your team work toward a mutually agreeable solution that will satisfy as much of everyone's needs as possible.

FIGURE 6–4

What Team Leaders and Facilitators Can Do to Help Teams Resolve Conflict

- Provide guidance and clear direction during the goal-setting process.

- Make sure the team develops guidelines for how it will function as a team.

- Use proven team processes, tools, and techniques for brainstorming, problem solving, decision making, and analysis. Using these methods helps teams address conflict naturally, as part of the process.

- Make sure people understand the various team roles (facilitator, leader, member, recorder, time keeper) and that these roles are carried out.

- Help the team determine whether a disagreement is central and important to the team's progress, or peripheral and therefore not important to the team's progress.

- Keep the team focused on its goal. When conflict arises, ask, "Does this need to be resolved for us to reach our goal?"

- When the team members get buried in conflict, refocus them on the end result. Ask, "What is our goal? What are we trying to achieve?"

- Help team members bring hidden agendas into the open.

LINK WITH OTHER TEAMS

Organizations have been investing in team training, team-building sessions, and resource materials for their employees in order to create self-directed teams that can assume the "whole job." They reinforce the concept of joining together in order to win—to experience production wins, sales wins, deadline wins, quality wins, service wins, profit wins.

In the quest to develop these teams with group unity, "us-versus-them" cultures emerge. The intent behind building these tight teams with unity is admirable: to help team members develop group identity and acquire confidence in each other's work. Team members work so hard, however, at winning that they fail to listen and learn from the other teams.

To avoid the pitfalls of competitive teaming, members should focus on shared accountability for the betterment of the whole. This requires linking with other teams and other parts of the organization. This also requires linkages with other organizations, customers, and vendors. *Three Levels of Teaming* (Figure 6–5) lists the characteristics required for Level C—shared teaming. (It is described in more detail in Chapter 4, "Assessing Team Requirements.")

This level of teaming will be increasingly necessary to align with the information society; a society of open communications, open system technology, and an open market. Yet self-directed, autonomous teams will also be necessary to assure a primary source of accountability for producing and measuring specified outcomes.

The dilemma for team members in the 1990s will be the ability to find a balance between self-directed teams and shared teaming. If your team needs to work at Level C, shared teaming, as well as Level B, self-directed teams, the challenge for you and your co-team members will be to determine how:

- Not to get "stuck" in Level B with so much "own team" identity that your team is viewed as uncooperative, a group of saboteurs, and/or out for your own team's gain at the expense of others.
- To obtain and maintain your own team cohesion while also working with other teams for shared learnings and experiences.

FIGURE 6-5

THREE LEVELS OF TEAMING: CHARACTERISTICS*†		
LEVEL A COHESIVE WORK GROUP *Group Work*	**LEVEL B** EFFICIENT WORK TEAM *Self-Directed Team*	**LEVEL C** EFFECTIVE ORGANIZATION UNIT *Shared Teaming*
Most required characteristics of a cohesive work group:	*Most required characteristics of an efficient work team:*	*Most required characteristics of an effective organizational unit:*
❏ Identification first with individual work and second with that of the group.	❏ High identification with own team.	❏ More awareness of other teams; less "own team" identity.
❏ Decision-making processes with individual and group input.	❏ Decision-making process shared among team members.	❏ Decision-making process shared between teams and with other parts of the organization.
❏ Formal communication sessions for sharing of group results. Minimal requirement for informal or spontaneous communication.	❏ Extensive feedback and clarification within own team. Frequent informal or spontaneous communication.	❏ Extensive use of intra- and interteam feedback and clarification. Communication in "our organization" terms.
❏ Segregated assignments with minimal sharing of work tasks or integrating work objectives.	❏ Common knowledge base among team members with work processes and production problems.	❏ Continuous checking of other teams' progress and realignment of the work.
❏ Comfortable group atmosphere.	❏ Unity and mutual support to defend team purpose and goals. "Our team" identity.	❏ General tone is collaborative for satisfaction of everyone in the organization, "betterment of the whole."
❏ Basic respect and mutual support for individuals' knowledge and skills.	❏ Mutual respect and admiration within team for accomplishment of shared goals.	❏ Conscious effort to build trust with other teams and other parts of the organization.
❏ Synergy from group recognition of individual contributions.	❏ Synergy from feelings of winning through accomplishment of "own team" goals.	❏ Synergy from feelings of winning through goal accomplishment for the total organization.

* This checklist is located in Appendix II: Checklists.

† Use this checklist to assess the level of teaming required.

- To assure you are doing more than just passing work off to the next part of the organization or another team; to be aware of what *others* need from your team so that they can more effectively do *their* work.

- To interface and develop alliances with customers, suppliers, other functions and teams to assure *your team* knows what *it* needs from them to improve *your team's* work processes and results.

Figures 6–6 and 6–7 provide intra- and interteam identification listings for you and your co-team members to use to determine if you have overidentified within your own team and may be failing to link with other teams. You may want to use these lists with another team or even a customer group. Ask them to review the two lists and share their perception of your team.

FIGURE 6-6

LEVEL B—EFFICIENT WORK TEAM

Efficient Work Team—Competitive Approach

❏ High identification with "own team"; polarization between teams.

❏ Decision making is in own team first and then shared with other teams.

❏ Limited feedback and clarification with other teams.

❏ Communication in "we–they" terms.

❏ Minimal cross-team sharing or integration of the work.

❏ Conflict with the "pass-off" of work processes and production expectations; hostility expressed toward other teams when expectations not met.

❏ Stress from assuming total accountability within own team, causing team isolation.

❏ Little information generated between teams.

❏ Mistrust of other teams; defensive of "own team."

❏ Subjectivity to defend "own team"; strong group identity.

❏ Reactive versus proactive to other teams' requests.

❏ Some teams win; some teams lose.

❏ Mutual admiration among team members for accomplishing team goals.

Intrateam Identification

FIGURE 6-7

LEVEL C—EFFICIENT ORGANIZATIONAL UNIT

Shared Teaming—Collaborative Approach

- ❏ More awareness of other groups; less "own team" identity.
- ❏ Decision-making methods agreed upon between teams and implemented.
- ❏ Extensive use of feedback and clarification with other teams.
- ❏ Communication in "we" terms.
- ❏ Continuous checking of other team's perceptions and realignment of the work between teams.
- ❏ Clarification of work processes, production expectations, and resources required by other teams.
- ❏ Stress as a result of implementing continuous problem solving.
- ❏ Large amount of information generated—sometimes overwhelming.
- ❏ Conscious effort to build trust between teams.
- ❏ General tone is objective for the benefit of the whole organization.
- ❏ Proactive—to promote interteam interface.
- ❏ Satisfaction for everyone—all winners; no superstars.
- ❏ Mutual support for accomplishment of all teams' goals.

Interteam Identification.

TEAM SITUATION

Two managing directors within the same software/hardware design division of a telecommunications company decided it would be more productive and cost effective to join together by implementing Integrated Product Development Teams (IPDTs) both within and between their two groups. Their two groups included the development and production aspects of the software design.

The directors introduced the concept and expectations by holding communication sessions with all employees. They assumed that their managers and employees would continue the shared communication sessions to institute working together and establishing integrated product teams.

TEAMS IN ACTION

One of the directors had been modeling the team concept and providing his 200 employees with team training for the past two years. This training was aimed at Level B for Efficient, Self-Directed Teams. As a result, strong semiautonomous teams were developed with their "own team" identity.

The other director, new to the division, had just begun to introduce the team concept. The majority of his group of approximately 80 employees had worked in the division for many years. It had been a traditional environment with individual work and directive management.

Confusion emerged as some employees began to practice the IPDT concept and others resisted. The two directors thought that the resistance was due to a lack of understanding about the benefits of teaming. To resolve this problem they reviewed—with the employees from both divisions—the following reasons for joining together:

- "We must learn to work differently to change from our prior, regulated environment, which provided guaranteed budgets and programs, to an entrepreneurial environment that is aggressive and progressive."

- "We need members of both divisions to share information with one another to complete our projects on schedule."

- "We are shifting to open systems technology with integrated processes. Our design and development work cannot be completed unless we provide cross-functional assistance throughout the divisions."

- "Both of our groups' technology requires that we secure and provide shared resources in order to complete our projects."

- "The scope of our work includes addressing issues and groups outside the organization (e.g., customers, vendors, and corporate entities)."

- "Much of our work has been contracted out. We must join together and prove that we can compete and remain in business with our development schedule, quality standards, and return on investment plan."

The two directors were admittedly dismayed to discover that this did not work and that the resistance continued to grow in some groups. Duplication of effort—because some teams were in place and others were not—added to the confusion in the work environment.

The directors provided facilitation training to help the teams with their planning and meetings and to resolve the resistance problem. Although this helped the meeting process and individuals felt more confident in group sessions, they (individuals and teams) rarely worked together with their daily assignments.

By this time, the directors realized that perhaps teaming was more difficult than they had anticipated. They remained committed to the IPDT concept and devised a more formal plan through a pilot team demonstration.

Team Process

Six Elements of Healthy Teamwork

A cross section of employees who needed to understand one another's work for planning and scheduling were invited to be part of a pilot IPDT to demonstrate the integrated team concept. An appointed team sponsor then selected 16 individuals to represent five different work units and three geographical locations. Two other divisional members who had received the facilitation training assisted the group along with an external consultant.

Even though their written invitation stated the purpose—to become a pilot team and receive team training—the members of this cross-functional team thought they were invited to a one-time meeting for planning and scheduling. They did not perceive themselves as members of a team, nor did they understand the need for team training. Their sponsor introduced them to the "Working Together" chapter of this book as a means to help them discover for themselves why they needed to function, at times, as an Integrated Product Development Team when working together as representatives of their various work units.

The Six Elements of Healthy Teamwork, defined earlier in this chapter, were reviewed to help the individual members discover their own resistance to shared planning and scheduling.

Process Steps:

1. Each person selects one of the six elements that he or she perceives the team members have in common and that supports the team's effectiveness—a group strength.

2. Each person selects one of the six elements that is *not* shared among all the individuals and without which effectiveness could be hindered—a group vulnerability.

3. Starting with the elements the members listed as strengths, each member reads to the group the one he or she selected and states why. (Record the selected elements and reasons on a large easel sheet for group memory.)

4. Each member shares the selected elements listed as vulnerabilities and states the reasons why. (Record on easel sheet for group memory.)

5. Review the lists; conduct a team dialog about the team's strengths and vulnerabilities.

6. Plan ways to build on the strengths and to problem solve on the vulnerabilities.

TEAM RESULTS

SIX ELEMENTS OF HEALTHY TEAMWORK

All 16 members selected the same group strength—mutual respect. They expressed mutual respect for one another's individual knowledge and expertise. The team discovered that they lacked five of the six elements, particularly emotional status, mutual support, and mutual celebration. Their team notes are illustrated in Figure 6–8.

The team members were pleased to learn that, in general, they were respectful of one another's abilities and knowledge. This enhanced both individual and group self-respect and confidence.

Discovering the lack of mutual support and concern for emotional status was a bit sobering for the team. This led to some sharing as to why they hadn't been supporting one another. They determined that job security issues were of concern because of recent company layoffs and outsourcing. They asked their team sponsor to clarify the current status. The team sponsor's explanation helped to minimize their concerns about job security, which allowed them to concentrate on becoming a cohesive team.

FIGURE 6–8
TEAMS IN ACTION
EXAMPLE: TEAM
NOTES

SIX ELEMENTS OF HEALTHY TEAMWORK

Group strengths

- *Mutual Respect*

  Recognize professional and expert knowledge and abilities

  Capabilities are there to deliver

  Ability and expertise

  Recognize expertise

  Skills and knowledge

Group vulnerabilities

- *Emotional status*

  Not sole team; lots of external forces that introduce conflict in goals

  Organizational changes future of the company; outsourcing of work

  Staffing exercises

  Rapid changes make us uncomfortable; not fun

- *Mutual support*

  Individuals have conflicting goals

  Working in silos

  Reluctance in getting involved

  Survival instinct

- *Mutual celebration*

  Little recognition

  Long projects; no time out to celebrate along the way versus at end

The team members agreed to build upon their group strength of mutual respect, learn more about one another's work responsibilities, and to develop mutual support.

TEAM PROCESS

TEAM DEVELOPMENT CYCLE "THE MAGIC CIRCLE"

Having identified the team's strengths and vulnerabilities, the team proceeded to address the lack of mutual support by identifying their team mission and goals. They referred to the material on Assessing

Team Requirements, which is presented in Chapter 4 of this book, to help assess the degree of teaming and support required. They acknowledged that there would be times when it would be appropriate to perform as a team rather than as individual contributors. They then used the *Three Levels of Teaming Checklist* (see Chapter 4) and determined that they needed to operate at Level C—shared teaming—when working on joint activities. They estimated that their joint activities for this requirement would be infrequent, however.

During the next team session the members reviewed the *Team Development Cycle* criteria presented in this chapter and acknowledged that their team probably lacked both membership and influence.

The *Magic Circle* exercise was used as a way of addressing their team membership and influence issues. The steps for the exercise follow.

Process Steps:

1. Draw a large circle on a piece of easel paper or use chalk to draw one on the floor. Draw three smaller circles in the larger circle, similar to a dart board.

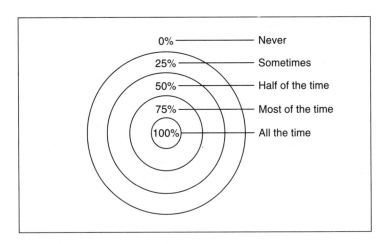

Mark percentages as shown on the illustration above. These percentages represent five categories as defined beside the illustration.

2. Each team member selects a token of some kind to identify him- or herself—a coffee cup, colored pen, piece of Post-It® note paper. If possible, it is preferable to have similar tokens for everyone, such as a colored circle with the team member's name printed on it.

3. Together, read the Membership and Influence definitions from the *Team Development Cycle.* Discuss the difference between membership in teams, which is the sense of belonging, versus influence, which is the belief that one can have an impact on the decisions of the team. Some people need to feel a sense of membership before they want to influence a group. Others need to perceive they can influence a group before they want to gain membership.

4. Begin with membership. At the count of three each person places his or her token on the *Magic Circle* according to his or her perceived membership in the team.

5. Conduct a team dialog about individual and collective membership.

> Address individual member's concerns, wishes, and issues.
>
> Each member shares and receives feedback.
>
> Discuss the team's membership in general.

6. Repeat the same process for influence.

> Simultaneously, everyone places his or her token according to his or her perception regarding influence.
>
> Each member shares and receives feedback.
>
> Close with overview on the team's influence in general.

7. Problem solve ways to ensure membership and influence. Everyone does not require the same degree. The goal is for each team member to feel a part of the team and able to contribute.

TEAM RESULTS

TEAM DEVELOPMENT CYCLE "THE MAGIC CIRCLE"

The *Magic Circle* exercise, illustrated in Figure 6–9, supported the notion that there was a general comfort level with membership. It helped the team recognize and confront their influence issue, how-ever, as the majority of their tokens were in the "25%—Sometimes" category. This further supported their findings from the *Six Elements of Healthy Teamwork*—that they respected one another's expertise and knowledge as individual contributors but lacked a value for *accepting* the expertise from one another. They made a ver-bal commitment with one another to continue meeting on a scheduled basis and to work towards more trust and influence.

FIGURE 6-9
TEAMS IN ACTION
EXAMPLE

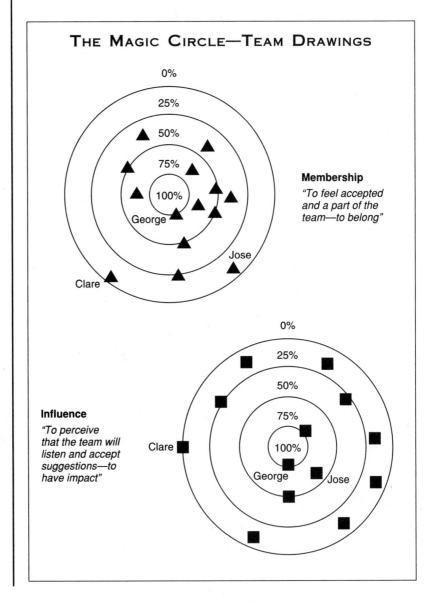

The group members continued their discussion with three individual situations that merited attention (see Figure 6–9):

- George perceived that he had full membership and influence. The team members, however, told him that he dominated the team, and that although they let him have control much of the time, they often did not accept his input to the degree he had assumed. They stated examples of George's dominance and offered to confront him in the future. He thanked the group for this new information about himself and agreed to be accepting of any future (constructive) criticism.

- Jose explained he was comfortable having placed his token on 25 percent. He felt this was representative of his membership on the team. He belongs to several community groups and has all the group membership he wants. He does not desire inclusion, as he would rather focus on team goals. He feels listened to and accepted by the team, which he does want. The team members accepted his explanation.

- Clare has felt rejected; she recently transferred into this division and feels her ideas are considered "from Mars." The team shared with her that they felt she was critical of this division's work and did not want to contribute. They felt rejected by Clare! They identified ways to include Clare and her ideas. They also designated a team member "buddy" to brief her on their organizational culture and its work history.

TEAM PROCESS
CONFLICT RESOLUTION

The team's consultant suggested that their commitment to build trust and influence may not be easy, and if not taken seriously might even cause some conflict. The *Model for Conflict Utilization* from this chapter was referenced. The team used the process steps that follow to perform an exercise to identify potential conflicts over information, methods, goals, and values. Figure 6–10 illustrates the areas of conflict they identified.

Process Steps:

1. As an entire team, brainstorm all the ways information might become a source of team conflict.

    List the ways.

    Problem solve how to avoid misinformation or misunderstandings about information.

2. Next, brainstorm how work and behavioral methods might cause team conflict.

    List types of work and behavioral methods.

    Agree upon work procedures that will be used as team methods.

    Establish team guidelines for team behaviors (See Chapter 3, "Organizing Teams").

3. Together, review team goals and discuss conflict over goals.

    What types of individual goals may conflict with these team goals.

    List examples of how team members may experience conflict over goals.

    Discuss ways to support one another with these conflicts.

4. Determine individual values that could impact work behaviors and team goals. Do this exercise in pairs.

    Prepare 10 small pieces of paper or 3" × 5" cards for each team member.

    Each person selects personal values and writes one on each card. These values should represent attributes, beliefs, goals, or dreams the person most desires.

    Indicate the priority of each value by numbering the cards from 1 to 10. Use the number 1 for the value most important to you and 10 for the value least important to you.

    Share your values with your partner, one person and one value at a time. Either person (Partner A) begins by presenting his or her values to the other person (Partner B). Start with the least important (number 10) and work through to the most important (number 1), explaining why each value is important to you.

After Partner A has shared all 10 of his or her values, Partner B takes each value card away from Partner A. Do this by making up a story to help Partner A feel the loss of each. (For example if the value is financial security, you could say "Your car broke down last night on the freeway, your mortgage is three months overdue, your health insurance has been cancelled, and you've heard a rumor that your job might be eliminated. You have spent all your savings. Your financial security is gone!"). Ask Partner A to share what the loss feels like.

Return the values by handing back the cards and retracting the stories, one by one.

Partner A shares how it feels to have each value returned.

Partner A then reviews and reprioritizes the 10 values based on new insights from this exercise.

Reverse roles and repeat the process with Partner B sharing his or her values.

CONFLICT IDENTIFICATION

Conflicts over goals that team members may experience
- Duplication
- Ownership
- Priorities
- Different tactics
- Expectations—set goals you can't obtain
- Measurability
- Timetable
- Quality

Values from which team may experience conflicts
- Code of ethics
- Work ethics
- Levels of integrity/honesty
- Importance of work
- Sense of timing
- Personal time
- Having fun
- Cultural/Religious differences
- View of authority

FIGURE 6–10 TEAMS IN ACTION EXAMPLE—TEAM NOTES

5. As a group, list the three highest prioritized values for each team member.

> Consider one another's three highest values. How similar or dissimilar are they?

> Discuss how each value might conflict with other team members and how different perceptions for the same value might occur.

> Strategize how to learn from and honor one another's values.

TEAM RESULTS

CONFLICT RESOLUTION

The team members listed their prioritized values and then discussed each value in terms of perceptions and expectations that might differ.

Some examples were:

- **Code of ethics.** The team members discussed codes of ethics from their respective functional organizations in regard to software documentation, copyright issues, and proprietary information. They then established a code of ethics for this cross-functional team to honor.
- **Having Fun.** There was quite a heated discussion about what fun means in a work environment. Some members believed fun does not fit at work. Others said they wouldn't work where there was no fun. They compromised and agreed to have nonwork lunch breaks and to meet at pleasant meeting places such as the local country club for their quarterly "off-sites" for their team fun.

Once each value was discussed, the team then reviewed both the goals and the values lists and pinpointed which ones might be the most likely to cause conflict. They then talked about how they would recognize when this started to occur. They also discussed how the conflict would jeopardize the team's mutual support as well as individual membership or influence.

In closing, they requested that the two trained facilitators continue to facilitate their team sessions and help them address and learn from the:

- Six Elements of Healthy Teamwork
- Team Development Cycle—The Magic Circle
- Conflict Resolution

CHAPTER SEVEN

BALANCING DIVERSITY

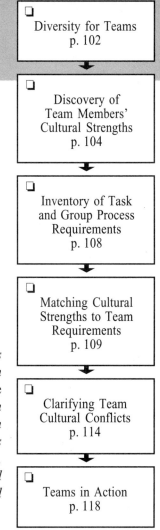

he Teams in Action *story for this chapter introduces a U.S–Mexico twin plant (maquiladora) that struggled through conflict to collaboration. You will see how they used the* Reverse Mirroring *process to address their key cultural issues and reach a new level of understanding, appreciation, and value for each other. Together, managers and technical staff from the two cultures created a flexible, productive, and cost-effective work environment, which performs at world-class manufacturing (WCM) levels and was the first Mexican manufacturing facility to win the coveted Shingo Award for Manufacturing Excellence.*

• • •

In today's highly competitive world, organizations can stumble and even cease to exist for failing to address and work toward cultural balance.

Culture embodies our personal values, life experiences and work expectations. It directly affects how we behave and how we respond to people and situations. All organizations develop cultures and subcultures that have this governing function. Some cultures work well with each other; others do not.

When cultures are balanced, which means that each person's uniqueness is respected and drawn upon to enrich the composition of the group, the team is stronger and more able to meet the agility required in today's marketplace. In turn, team members feel more valued and satisfied with their team contributions.

When cultures do not *work* well together, suspicion, hostility, and stereotyping often enter the environment. When not addressed, these conditions can lead to a lack of mobility, both of people and ideas. People, feeling threatened by new ideas, often become more concerned with their own identity and survival than with other team members and the customer. This response leads to decreased performance for the organization.

Addressing and achieving cultural balance is neither magical nor difficult. Rather, it takes leadership, persistence, and a strong desire for people to work more effectively. The examples, processes, and methods presented in this chapter are designed to give you and your co-team members encouragement and practical results.

This chapter provides four practical processes, including examples, for balancing your team's diversity:

1. Discovering team members' cultural strengths.
2. Inventory of task and group process requirements.
3. Matching cultural strengths with team requirements.
4. Understanding diversities at a deeper level by clarifying team cultural conflicts.

DIVERSITY FOR TEAMS

Definitions of the following three terms are needed to help you and your co-team members achieve a balance in your team diversity:

- Cultural diversity
- Team diversity
- Team balance

What Is Cultural Diversity?

Culture includes those attributes that can uniquely be ascribed to individuals, teams, functions, organizations, regions, countries, and races. Culture sets bounds on what people believe, how the world is seen, and what is deemed acceptable and unacceptable. Cultural diversity is the recognition that these differences are valuable. It presupposes that by developing these differences as cultural strengths, a wider array of approaches and choices are available to everyone.

Teams perform best when all members feel they have equal value. For years, this sense of equality was based upon people becoming as much like one another as possible. Current demands for broader team responsibilities create opportunities for equality by requiring different approaches, diverse ways of thinking, and a variety of competencies for doing the work.

What Is Team Diversity?

Team diversity means using the collective differences of team members to get the work done. For many organizations, developing team diversity has progressed far beyond quotas and sensitivity training and has become a core business strategy.

The diversity of your team members represents a tremendous reservoir of talent waiting to be tapped. Some of the differences that will have a positive impact when valued and balanced within a team include:

- Age and lifetime experiences and exposure.
- Family experience—large, small, close knit, formal, informal, nuclear, extended.
- Ethnic background, native language, cultural exposure, and race.
- Education—formal and informal.
- Social and community involvement—associations, sports, churches, social halls, or clubs.
- Perceived societal roles and expectations.
- Disabilities and health restrictions.

- Work experiences—shifts and schedules; types of assignments; and sizes and types of companies, such as government, industrial, or small business.
- Tenure—length of time in the assignment or work area.
- Professional and vocational interests, knowledge, and skills.
- Preferred WorkStyle or way of working.

WHAT IS TEAM BALANCE?

Teams are designing, building, delivering, and supporting products and services that serve a more diverse set of customers. Teams can better address this expanded role by tapping the breadth of team members' cultural strengths—knowledge, skills, attributes, work approaches, and interests.

Balancing team diversity is defined as recognizing and taking the necessary steps to link the breadth of team members' cultural strengths to meet the team's purpose.

Teams may need to overcome a variety of divisions and barriers in order to address this balance. Many teams may not perceive the need among their members for mutual dependence, respect, and care for one another, but these are the underpinnings of true team balancing.

When team members' unique cultural strengths are valued and utilized by the other team members, team balance is achieved through a blending of those cultural strengths.

DISCOVERY OF TEAM MEMBERS' CULTURAL STRENGTHS

The team's discovery goal is to uncover and learn more about its members' backgrounds. Because people are hesitant to explore their personal differences in group settings, the following three steps can help make the discovery process a positive experience. These steps can be conducted in a day-long, off-site team development session or may be conducted as a series of two- or three-hour sessions.

1. REVIEW TEAM'S CHARTER

Begin the discovery by focusing on the purpose and work of the team itself. Do this by reviewing your team's charter, mission, goals, and role. Post the charter in a place where every team member can see it. *You will find that it is easier to share personal information when it is placed within the framework of your team's purpose.* (See Chapter 3, "Organizing Teams," for charter steps.)

Arrange for an outside facilitator to guide the first few sessions. Find someone who has worked with different cultures, is sensitive to individual feelings, and has group facilitation skills. Record each session's key points, having team members take turns with the recording role. (See Chapter 5, "Understanding Team Support Roles," for guidelines and checklists of facilitator and recorder roles.)

2. INTERVIEW EACH OTHER

The goal in interviewing each other is to find out the many different ways each of you can contribute to the team's mission.

Either on flip-chart paper or in handouts, have the following questions in a place where all team members can refer to them. Select a partner whom you do not know very well. Interview your partner using some of the questions from the following list and record your partner's responses. Read your notes back to your partner to confirm that you have recorded accurately. Later, record key points on large flip-chart paper to present to the rest of the team.

Early life experiences:

- Where did you grow up—in a rural, suburban, or urban area? What part of the country (or other countries) was this?

- How large was your family or extended family? Were you the oldest, youngest, or in between? How many brothers and sisters did you grow up with?

- Who influenced you the most as you were growing up, and how?

- As you were growing up, did you participate in any team activities such as sports, school, community, or church groups?
- In what ways did your family operate as a team—family business, dinner table sharing, family gatherings, vacations?

School, work, and adult life experiences:

- In school or educational settings, were you exposed to differences that you had not been aware of before? In what ways did this affect your thinking or perceptions of others?
- What were your early work experiences—for example, a summer job or volunteer assignment? From these, what did you learn about yourself and about work?
- In your adult work experiences, have you learned anything else about yourself and about work?
- How about travel or living experiences in different neighborhoods or countries? Did you gain any insights about your values and beliefs and those of others?
- Did you ever, in school, at work, or in a community, experience any prejudice or rejection due to being or feeling culturally different?

Experiences with this team:

- What would you like to contribute to the team's work that you may not have had the opportunity to do in the past?
- How does the work of this team fit into your personal goals and what is important to you?
- Are there any perceptions or cultural issues that might prevent you from feeling ready to fully contribute to the team at this time?

3. Validate Each Other

Introduce each other to the whole team by summarizing what you learned about your partner from the questions. After the information is shared, validate the person's potential contributions to the group by having the team members summarize what they perceive to be their partner's cultural strengths. Help each person discover that what may have been considered a conflicting difference before is now a vital contribution. (See Figure 7–1, *Cultural Strengths Worksheet.*)

Now you have taken the first step in discovering the diversity of interests, attributes, and experiences the members of your team have to offer. Your next step is to inventory what the team's work requirements will be to support the team mission.

FIGURE 7–1

CULTURAL STRENGTHS WORKSHEET EXAMPLE

Samantha's cultural strengths	Team needs Samantha can contribute to:
Helped to raise siblings, is sensitive to feelings and relationships; sees this as important in teams, too.	_____ _____
Whole-picture thinking; concern for quality standards; wants things done right.	_____ _____
Care for individual welfare; volunteers in a community center.	_____ _____
Comfortable expressing her observations and opinions; raised in extended family; learned how to be seen and heard.	_____ _____
Grew up in a rough neighborhood; wants upward mobility and improved lifestyle.	_____ _____
Likes to read and write; obtaining further education.	_____ _____

Inventory of Task and Group Process Requirements

To complete the inventory process, make a list of your team's task and group process requirements. To start, discuss the difference between *task* and *group process* requirements, using these definitions:

- **Task** requirements are those activities required to perform the work itself; these activities are in support of the team mission.

- **Group process** represents behavioral and operational activities that support getting the work done—things team members do to support the content of their work. (See Figure 7–2 for generic examples.)

FIGURE 7–2

Team Requirements: Task and Group Process Example

Typical team task requirements (specific to a manufacturing team)	Typical group process requirements (applicable for any team)
Precision assembly.	Problem identification and solving.
Solder parts.	Relationship building between members and with suppliers and customers.
Inspect product.	
Correct and document quality errors.	Shared planning and scheduling.
Monitor for possible machine malfunction.	Data gathering and reporting back to the team.
Fill out reports.	Maintenance of team morale.
Install and test new equipment.	Positioning the team's recommendations with other teams.
Collect and synthesize process control data.	
Package and deliver products.	Decision making.
	Conflict resolution within the team.

1. List Requirements

As you did with the first discovery step, locate an outside facilitator and internal recorder to help you. Use group brainstorming to list as many task and group process requirements as you can. Create a separate flip-chart page for each list. Refer to your team's charter as you develop your lists. You may discover that a true separation between the team's tasks and group processes will be difficult to discern. Do your best, but don't waste time trying to be absolutely correct!

2. Evaluate Requirements

Evaluate how well you and your co-team members are meeting your team requirements. After completing the two lists and implementing the requirements into your team's work, consider your performance as a team by evaluating each task and group process requirement with a grading system. Select a system comfortable for the team (for example, A, B, C; or +, –). It is important for all members to be honest and willing to challenge one another with this evaluation.

3. Review and Prepare

By challenging yourselves to consider your team's performance, you are now in a position to identify team members' cultural strengths that are contributing to the team's success as well as those strengths that could be better utilized to support the team. Discuss examples of cultural strengths in your team.

Each member should prepare for the next session by giving thought to matching the team members' diverse strengths to the team's task and group process requirements. Consider all team members but in particular remember the person you interviewed earlier.

Matching Cultural Strengths to Team Requirements

Once you have completed an inventory of your team's diversity and individual cultural strengths as well as your team task and process requirements, you are ready to take the final step of matching the requirements with strengths. Use the following five steps to help ensure your success and guide you and your co-team members to practical applications.

1. SET UP MEETING SPACE

As before, outside facilitation and internal recording will help the process. All team members should have access to the prior lists of member cultural strengths and team task and group process requirements. You can do this by using handouts or flip-chart easel sheets.

2. ESTABLISH TEAM BALANCE GOAL

To obtain a balance of cultural strengths with your team's diversity, consider possible linkages between members' cultural strengths and your team's task and group process requirements. Together with your co-team members, create a statement that reflects your team balance goal. An example of such a goal might be:

> Our goal in this session is to find ways to link people's unique strengths with what we need to do as a team. This is an exploration to consider how we can utilize our cultural strengths, it won't be cast in concrete.
>
> The fact that someone expresses an interest or has past experience in a particular area, activity, or concept does not automatically mean he or she should always represent that subject or do that activity.
>
> *This doesn't mean that people keep doing the same things just because they always have, either. Balance is what works for both the team and the team member. Balance is derived from awareness and the opportunity to practice.*

As a team member, you should feel comfortable that this is first an exploration process. Neither you nor your co-team members will be stereotyped. If this is happening, say so. Then ask the team why this might be happening. How could you or the co-team members be perceived differently? (See Fig. 7–3, *Cultural Strengths Worksheet*).

FIGURE 7-3

CULTURAL STRENGTHS WORKSHEET

Samantha's cultural strengths	Team needs Samantha can contribute to:
Helped to raise siblings, is sensitive to feelings and relationships; sees this as important in teams, too.	*Members' relationship building Supplier and customer relationship building*
Whole-picture thinking; concern for quality standards; wants things done right.	*Process controls and quality*
Care for individual welfare; volunteers in a community center.	*Team's morale*
Comfortable expressing her observations and opinions; raised in extended family; learned how to be seen and heard.	*Work through conflicts*
Grew up in a rough neighborhood; wants upward mobility and improved lifestyle.	*Decision making*
Likes to read and write; obtaining further education.	*Fill out reports, document errors, data gathering*

3. IDENTIFY STRENGTHS AND REQUIREMENTS

Start with the positive by identifying where and how members are currently contributing to the identified team task and group process and relate those contributions to each team member's cultural strengths.

Example 1: Relationship Building Is a Group Process Requirement

Contribution: Samantha has been an influential force in relationship building for team unity; she has organized several potluck lunches and hosted a team gathering at her home.

Cultural Strength: Samantha is sensitive to feelings and relationships.

Documentation: Record "Relationship building between members" on Samantha's chart next to her strength of being "Sensitive to feelings and relationships." Record Samantha's name under the team process requirement of "Relationship Building." (See Fig. 7–2, *Team Requirements: Task and Group Process,* and 7–3, *Cultural Strengths Worksheet Example.*)

After you and your co-team members have processed the team's task and group process strengths and related them to your members' attributes, focus on the team requirements that might need improvement. Some members may currently be making contributions in requirement areas needing improvement, but these areas might need contributions from others as well.

Example 2: Task Requirement to Collect and Synthesize Process Control Data

Contribution: The quality of the team's output could improve if we utilize Samantha's ability to see the whole picture on process controls, which is combined with her concern for quality.

Attribute: Samantha thinks about the whole picture and has a concern for quality.

Documentation: Record "Process controls and quality" on Samantha's chart next to her strength of "Whole-picture thinking; concern for quality standards" and record Samantha's name under the group process requirement of "Process Controls and Quality." (See Figure 7–2, *Team Requirements: Task and Group Process.*)

4. Summarize Discoveries

Chances are that you and your co-team members may have a different view of yourselves as a result of this matching exercise. You will need to take a few moments to discuss this experience and then find ways to allow the discoveries to become reality and a part of your team culture. Consider the following questions during your group discussion:

- Did you learn something new about yourself?

- Did you learn something new about another team member?

- Are there cultural strengths that you did not previously—but do now—perceive to be important for your team's success?

- Are there cultural strengths that your team needs more of or that your team may lack and could benefit from if made more available?

Understanding and utilization of each other's cultural strengths will happen spontaneously as team members experience greater acceptance and support for initiating ideas, inquiries, and actions.

Document the results from each of the exercises: Discovery of Team Members' Cultural Strengths, Inventory of Task and Group Process Requirements, and Matching Cultural Strengths to Team Requirements. Give a copy to each team member and make the notes a part of the team's history.

5. Celebrate!

Your team's cultural strengths—when focused, balanced, and working toward a common goal—will guarantee your team's future success. As members more fully contribute what they uniquely have to offer, positive results will flow (solutions will be found, goals will be met, and customers will be satisfied). Make a conscious effort to recognize one another's unique contributions, because together you make the difference.

CLARIFYING TEAM CULTURAL CONFLICTS

REVERSE MIRRORING PROCESS[2]

At times, teams enter into an awareness of diversity through the "back door" by addressing a specific conflict. As the working world becomes smaller and more interdependent, "micro cultures," which previously existed at a distance from each other, often clash as they begin to work more closely together. The following examples and the *Reverse Mirroring* process that accompanies them may vary from your specific circumstance; the methods, however, can be readily applied to your situation.

Examples of Team Cultural Conflicts

Functional Conflicts

Research & Development	versus	Manufacturing
Sales	versus	Marketing
Retail	versus	Wholesale
Finance	versus	Procurement

Values Conflicts

College Degree	versus	"Street Smart"
Career	versus	Family
Individual Work	versus	Teamwork
Initiate	versus	Respond
Conservative	versus	Liberal
Nationality	versus	Nationality

Hierarchical Conflicts

Corporate Headquarters	versus	Regional Offices
Management	versus	Nonmanagement
Union Workers	versus	Nonunion Workers

Conflicts even emerge between teams in the same organization, division, department, or shift. The following steps outline a *Reverse Mirroring* exercise to uncover the roots underlying many team cultural conflicts.

1. PREPARATION

You will need an experienced facilitator to gain the greatest value from this exercise. Use flip charts and select someone to record the session. Plan on a minimum of two hours and a maximum of four

---

[2]Concept credit: W. J. Crockett

hours to conduct the first session. Planning and preparation prior to the first session are also helpful.

2. CULTURAL CONFLICT IDENTIFICATION

Where do you start when you suspect that cultural issues—the values, beliefs, or norms of any single group or function—are at the heart of the conflict within or between teams? Acknowledge it; start talking about what you are experiencing. Acknowledgement gets the process started and creates the opportunity for broader awareness.

The *Reverse Mirroring* process is divided into four parts:

1. How we see ourselves.
2. How we see them
   (the "them" needs to be identified clearly).
3. How we think they see us.
4. How they think we see them.

Identify the cultural differences by types of strengths and by those members who best represent these cultural strengths. Include at least two members of each cultural subgroup; the subgroups represent differing cultural strengths. Select those who have knowledge about and experience regarding the conflict. They may not fully understand it, but at least they can express what the concerns are.

3. CULTURAL VALUES IDENTIFICATION

Begin by determining and reviewing the purpose of cultural clarification. This exercise can range from an initial discovery session to a more thorough understanding of the common values to a concerted effort to create a new hybrid culture.

- Discuss the overall purpose and obtain each team member's expectations.
- Hand out the *Reverse Mirroring Worksheet* (see Appendix II–9) and review the process steps. The *Teams in Action* story at the end of this chapter provides an example for this exercise.
- Separate into the two subgroups to work independently, and complete the worksheet. Do this together in your

subgroup and record your responses to each of the four statements on a flip chart—one page per quadrant of the worksheet.

To share the perceptions of each subgroup, establish a dialogue process in which one subgroup reports first and then becomes the focus for sharing with the other subgroup. The subgroup will share all four quadrants of the *Reverse Mirroring Values Worksheet,* and in turn receive perceptions from the other subgroup.

4. REVERSE MIRRORING DIALOG

Using the worksheet (see Figure 7–4), talk about the meaning of the different perceptions, and note where there are similarities and differences between them.

- Subgroup I, post your results from all four quadrants. Leave space for the other subgroup to place theirs, as illustrated below with the worksheets of Subgroup I and Subgroup II:

FIGURE 7–4

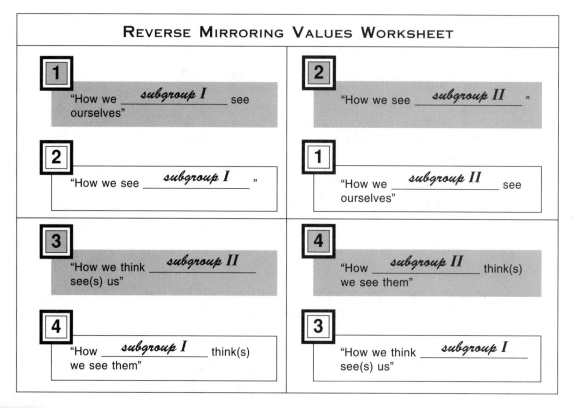

CHAPTER SEVEN

- Use colored markers to highlight statements that are similar from the two sets of perceptions and discuss why you perceive these similarities. These represent cultural strengths that both subgroups value and can build upon.

- With a different colored marker, highlight statements that are dissimilar and discuss why you perceive these differences. These represent cultural strengths that may need demonstration and practice over time to obtain shared understanding and value from all team members.

- Reverse the process and discuss Subgroup II's results from all four quadrants. Conduct a similar dialog with Subgroup II.

5. VALUES ACCEPTANCE

Conflicts over values and beliefs take time to resolve. Commitment to learn about and understand the values of another cultural strength is the first step. Acceptance follows understanding. The *Reverse Mirroring* process provides a framework for understanding. Acceptance can then be joined through the team's experiencing tangible benefits in meeting its work requirements. (See the section in Chapter 6, "Working Together," on *Resolving Team Conflict* for conflict resolution suggestions.)

- Identify one or two cultural strengths per subgroup that the other subgroup is willing to learn more about and that would benefit team requirements.

- Next, plan how the cultural strength can be utilized in the work of the team and how it will be appraised for its contribution to team results.

- Establish a date or method to revisit the *Reverse Mirroring* process. Discuss the benefits that have resulted and how these benefits have affected the team's success.

TEAMS IN ACTION

TEAM SITUATION

This team situation introduces the history, processes, and results of two cultures moving from conflict to collaboration. Using the tools and processes described in this chapter, the organization successfully learned to bridge its culture gap, creating a successful teamwork environment that consistently meets world-class manufacturing requirements.

An electronic assembly plant on the U.S.–Mexico border was struggling to have its people work as a team toward the same objectives. Poor relationships between the American managerial and technical staff and their Mexican counterparts created problems with product quality, cycle time, and operating costs.

The Americans believed that production was always in a state of crisis and always last minute. Additionally, they thought the cost in scrap and rework was unacceptably high. The Mexicans believed the Americans didn't truly value them for their abilities. They felt the Americans were demanding and always making more rules. Each group was quickly becoming the other's worst enemy.

TEAM PROCESS

Under the American plant manager's leadership, the 22 managers and engineers from both cultures agreed to attend a one-day session focusing on culture. The group was divided according to nationality: Mexican and American. Both groups worked separately using the *Reverse Mirroring* process (see p. 111 for a description of the process and see Figures 7–5 and 7–6 for each group's results).

Process Steps:

1. Each individual identifies subgroup culture and separates and records responses to complete the *Reverse Mirroring Values Worksheet* (see Appendix II–9). (Use one easel sheet per statement.)

2. Convene and share perspectives from the lists in a dialog process.

3. Compare similarities and differences in perceptions.

4. Create shared understanding of how to utilize the balanced strengths to create a blended culture.

FIGURE 7-5
TEAMS IN ACTION EXAMPLE

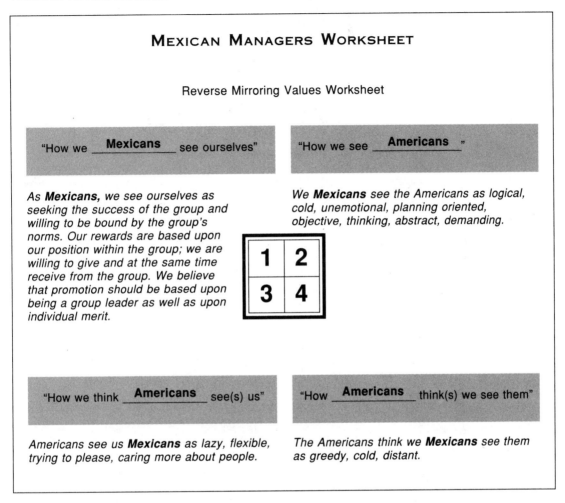

MEXICAN MANAGERS WORKSHEET

Reverse Mirroring Values Worksheet

"How we _____**Mexicans**_____ see ourselves"

"How we see _____**Americans**_____ "

As **Mexicans,** we see ourselves as seeking the success of the group and willing to be bound by the group's norms. Our rewards are based upon our position within the group; we are willing to give and at the same time receive from the group. We believe that promotion should be based upon being a group leader as well as upon individual merit.

We **Mexicans** see the Americans as logical, cold, unemotional, planning oriented, objective, thinking, abstract, demanding.

1	2
3	4

"How we think _____**Americans**_____ see(s) us"

"How _____**Americans**_____ think(s) we see them"

Americans see us **Mexicans** as lazy, flexible, trying to please, caring more about people.

The Americans think we **Mexicans** see them as greedy, cold, distant.

FIGURE 7-6
TEAMS IN ACTION EXAMPLE

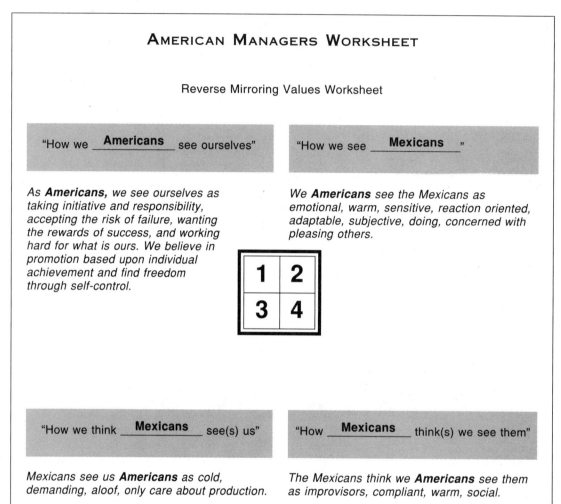

AMERICAN MANAGERS WORKSHEET

Reverse Mirroring Values Worksheet

"How we ___Americans___ see ourselves"

As **Americans,** we see ourselves as taking initiative and responsibility, accepting the risk of failure, wanting the rewards of success, and working hard for what is ours. We believe in promotion based upon individual achievement and find freedom through self-control.

"How we see ___Mexicans___"

We **Americans** see the Mexicans as emotional, warm, sensitive, reaction oriented, adaptable, subjective, doing, concerned with pleasing others.

1	2
3	4

"How we think ___Mexicans___ see(s) us"

Mexicans see us **Americans** as cold, demanding, aloof, only care about production.

"How ___Mexicans___ think(s) we see them"

The Mexicans think we **Americans** see them as improvisors, compliant, warm, social.

TEAM RESULTS

After completing the four questions individually, the group reconvened to share their responses. Both groups discovered that they had many values in common and that they were most critical of their own culture. Both groups also realized that the manufacturing plant needed core values from both cultures in order to succeed. As a result, the group of 22 American and Mexican managers created a filosofia (philosophy) statement that incorporated both sets of values:

> "We believe that our continued existence as an organization is dependent upon quality excellence and productivity improvement. We also believe that effective working relationships characterized by good communication, respect, trust, and honesty will improve product quality and productivity."

Since 1982, this filosofia statement has served as the foundation and framework for running the factory. The statement has a balanced concern for people as well as product quality and productivity. By focusing on people; developing, training, and treating all employees like professionals; and then expecting them to solve product and customer problems; all parties win.

New employees are screened for their ability to work in this kind of balanced culture where employees are expected to be bilingual—capable of interfacing with North American and European counterparts; where engineers are expected to be trainers and coaches rather than experts; and where teams form and disband naturally.

The plant has continually set cycle-time and cost-reduction records, expanded its product lines, and gone through a change in corporate ownership. In the midst of this change, the employees remain committed to their unique cultural strengths and value of people.

CHAPTER EIGHT

RUNNING TEAM MEETINGS

❏
Plan Team Meeting p. 124

↓

❏
Run Team Meeting p. 128

↓

❏
Document Team Meeting p. 130

↓

❏
Assign Action Plan p. 133

↓

❏
Evaluate Meeting Results p. 135

↓

❏
Teams in Action p. 137

The Teams in Action *in this chapter tells of a marketing staff group that so disliked meetings they quit having them. The lack of staff meetings caused communications issues in this department. Staff meetings were reinstituted using external facilitation help. This enabled the group to learn how to make meetings work.*

• • •

Meetings have become almost synonomous with teamwork. A meeting can function as a powerful mechanism to share information and to make group decisions. Meetings, however, can become a nuisance and a distraction from accomplishing work if they are used to excess or run ineffectively. People feel productive and rewarded for participating in a meeting when the appropriate members are involved, it is effectively facilitated with a clear purpose, and absorbs only the amount of time required to reach the necessary conclusion or resolution.

Meetings take on a number of forms, including stand-up up-dates, large group briefings, problem solving sessions, information sharing times, and think tank "free-for-alls." They can be conducted in many ways: face-to-face round tables, teleconferences, written round robins, or even via E-mail.

Generally speaking, a successful meeting:

- Provides an avenue to complete a task requiring input and resolution from a variety of people.

- Obtains commitment on the part of all participants to follow through on the decisions made.

- Allows people to interact at a deeper level and to develop working relationships.

PLAN TEAM MEETING

Before you have a team meeting, do the following:

- Determine objectives and agenda.

- Determine whether to use a team facilitator (see Figure 8–1, *Checklist for Determining Facilitator Requirements,* on page 125).

- Determine whether to use a subject matter expert or other assistance.

- Determine date, time, place.

- Notify all meeting participants.

- Secure supplies and equipment (See Figure 8–2, *Supplies, Facilities and Equipment Checklist,* on page 126.)

- Review how to begin a meeting (See Figure 8–3, *Checklist for Opening and Closing Team Meetings,* on page 127).

FIGURE 8-1

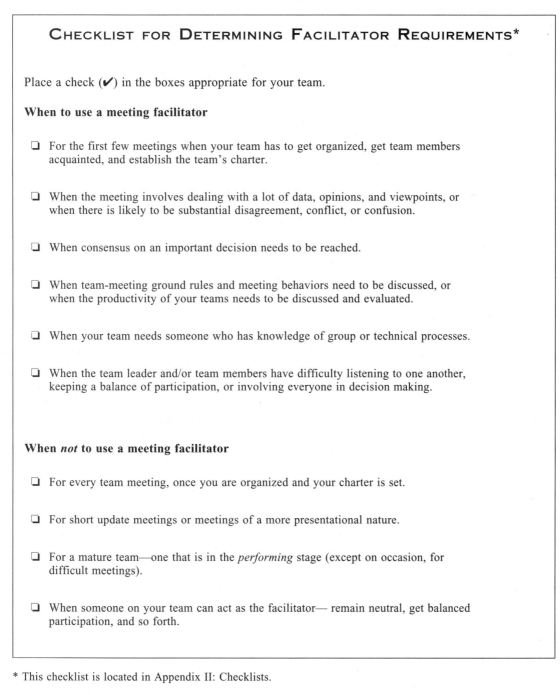

CHECKLIST FOR DETERMINING FACILITATOR REQUIREMENTS*

Place a check (✔) in the boxes appropriate for your team.

When to use a meeting facilitator

❏ For the first few meetings when your team has to get organized, get team members acquainted, and establish the team's charter.

❏ When the meeting involves dealing with a lot of data, opinions, and viewpoints, or when there is likely to be substantial disagreement, conflict, or confusion.

❏ When consensus on an important decision needs to be reached.

❏ When team-meeting ground rules and meeting behaviors need to be discussed, or when the productivity of your teams needs to be discussed and evaluated.

❏ When your team needs someone who has knowledge of group or technical processes.

❏ When the team leader and/or team members have difficulty listening to one another, keeping a balance of participation, or involving everyone in decision making.

When *not* to use a meeting facilitator

❏ For every team meeting, once you are organized and your charter is set.

❏ For short update meetings or meetings of a more presentational nature.

❏ For a mature team—one that is in the *performing* stage (except on occasion, for difficult meetings).

❏ When someone on your team can act as the facilitator— remain neutral, get balanced participation, and so forth.

* This checklist is located in Appendix II: Checklists.

FIGURE 8-2

SUPPLIES, FACILITIES AND EQUIPMENT CHECKLIST*

Place a check (✔) in the box once you have located an item.

You will need the following for most of your team meetings and other work:

❑ Flip chart easel and paper. (White board space is adequate for most team meetings.)

❑ Marking pens (be sure there are plenty).

    Water-based (don't bleed through onto walls).

    Use those meant for paper (not white boards).

    Have three or four different colors for highlighting, organizing.

    Mr. Sketch (scented) are easy to use; El Marko makes a good water-based pen.

    Use darkest colors for main text, lighter/brighter colors for highlighting.

❑ Pencils.

❑ Scissors.

❑ Masking tape (for posting flip charts on walls).

❑ Overhead projector, projector pens, transparencies, and screen (White wall space can be used in place of screen.)

❑ Blank forms (such as action planning forms, meeting evaluation forms, etc.).

❑ Note paper.

❑ Post It Notes.

❑ *Teaming by Design* (for reference).

❑ Copies of appropriate documentation:

    Action items from previous meeting.

    Information, data, and anything else that team members will need to keep informed and make decisions.

❑ Meeting space (comfortable and adequate).

* This checklist is located in Appendix II: Checklists.

FIGURE 8-3

CHECKLIST FOR OPENING AND CLOSING TEAM MEETINGS*

Place a check (✔) in the boxes appropriate for your team.

How to open a team meeting

❑ Start on time.

❑ Introduce any meeting guests.

❑ Review the charter, mission, and guidelines.

❑ Post meeting objectives/purpose and the agenda.

❑ Check to see if everyone agrees to the purpose and the agenda.

❑ Add agenda items as necessary, but keep meeting time limit in mind. Begin list of agenda items for future meetings.

❑ Review meeting ground rules the team has agreed upon.

❑ Announce who will be the recorder.

How to close a team meeting

❑ Allow 15–20 minutes to close the meeting (longer for lengthy, involved meetings).

❑ Post and review all decisions made and check for buy-in and understanding.

❑ Ask, "What action items have we agreed to / do we need to agree to?"

❑ Post all action items with **who** will do **what** by **when.** Check for buy-in.

❑ Set the next meeting time and date if possible.

❑ Review the collected list of issues and agenda items for future meetings. Get team's input on important items for upcoming meetings.

❑ Thank people for coming.

❑ End on time.

❑ From time to time, evaluate your team's meeting using the *Checklist for Successful Meetings.*

---

* This checklist is located in Appendix II: Checklists.

Make Sure Resources Are Available at Team Meetings

Just who is responsible for seeing that a meeting room has been reserved and the appropriate supplies are at the meeting site? What follows is a practical guideline.

Type of Meeting	Who Is Responsible
Team meeting	Team leader
Cross-functional meetings	Facilitator
Interteam meetings	Facilitator
Management meetings	Facilitator
Team's presentation to management or other teams	Team leader

Make sure it is clear whose responsibility it is to:

- Decide the date, time, and place of the meeting.
- Reserve the meeting room.
- Notify the participants/team members.
- Order and bring the flip chart, easel, marking pens, etc. to the meeting. (See Figure 8–2.)

One way to make sure responsibilities are clear is to use the *Action Plan* form near the end of this chapter (see Figure 8–7) and show each of the items on the previous list as action items on this form. Give those with meeting responsibilities a copy of the completed form.

Run Team Meeting

The team meeting agenda provides the framework for the session and the focus for the content. There are three typical times during which agendas are prepared:

1. During the beginning of team meetings.
2. Between meetings, by a designated team member, with distribution to the members prior to the next meeting.
3. At the close of a team meeting in order to plan the next meeting.

The *Team Meeting Agenda Format* (Figure 8–4) lists items to be included on an agenda.

FIGURE 8-4

TEAM MEETING AGENDA FORMAT

1. Introductions; brief updates since last session.
2. Review meeting objectives and agenda.
3. Establish priorities and time allotments for agenda items.
4. Review action items from last meeting.
5. New data/information.
6. Progress through agenda.
7. Summarize meeting decisions and action items.
8. Plan between-session actions.
9. Outline agenda for next meeting.
10. Conduct discussion on the process of the meeting; plan improvements for next meetings.

THINGS TO ACCOMPLISH AT THE FIRST MEETINGS

At the team's first meetings, team members will get acquainted and write the team charter. *These first few meetings are critical to the team's getting off to a good start and to its success as a team.*

Some of the *tasks* that need to be accomplished during the first meetings are:

- Clarification of team roles (leader, facilitator, etc.). Explanation of each role.
- Making a list of names, which includes team members, leader, facilitator, and so forth. Include phone, fax, building and mail stop numbers plus E-mail addresses so team members can contact one another.
- Completion of the team charter.
- Setting up initial meeting times and places; determine best way to communicate with one another between meetings, and discuss what to do if someone cannot attend a meeting. (Facilitator and team leader should emphasize importance of attendance at team meetings.)

Some of the *social* aspects that need to be covered at the first meetings are:

- Getting Acquainted: Allow time for members to get acquainted; design this into the meeting plan. (This was discussed in more detail in Chapters 3 and 7, "Organizing the Team" and "Balancing Diversity.")
- Team Membership: Allow members to learn why others were selected for the team; establish individual credibility.

DOCUMENT TEAM MEETING

Teams typically use one of the following methods to document the team's work. Both methods have advantages and disadvantages.

- Flip chart transcription
- Recorder-composed documentation

FLIP CHART TRANSCRIPTION

The team recorder (or facilitator or team leader) notes the agenda, decisions, main points, and action items on flip charts as the meeting progresses. These are posted for all to see. After the meeting, the charts are typed and copies distributed to all team members.

Advantages:
- Gives a fairly accurate picture of how the meeting progressed and what was said.
- Gives members a chance to check the data to see if it represents what was intended.
- Everyone sees the minutes (in flip chart form) before they leave the meeting, so there are no surprises.
- Recorder has the simple job of transcribing the charts.

Disadvantages:
- Charts are cumbersome.
- Requires a skilled recorder to accurately record meeting points.

- People who were not in attendance may have difficulty understanding the minutes.

RECORDER-COMPOSED DOCUMENTATION

The team recorder takes notes during the meeting, writes them or inputs them in a laptop computer, and then distributes them afterward in the form of "minutes."

Advantages:

- No cumbersome charts.
- Minutes can be made more understandable to those not present.

Disadvantages:

- Less opportunity for members to see and buy into what goes in the minutes.
- No notes for members to refer back to during the meeting.
- Recorder must spend time composing minutes, as opposed to transcribing charts.
- More risk of points being missed, changed, or editorialized by the recorder; less team ownership of the minutes.

WHAT TO INCLUDE IN TEAM MEETING MINUTES

Below is a suggested list of what to include in team meeting minutes, whether you are using the flip chart or the recorder-composed method.

- *Members present.*
- *Meeting objectives:* what you plan to accomplish at the meeting.
- *Agenda:* the flow of topics and activities to support your objectives.
- *Discussion:* main points and ideas, brief phrases to capture main ideas for each topic discussed.

- *Decisions made:* for each decision, write a statement that accurately represents the decisions your team has agreed upon.
- *Action items:* the next steps that will be taken to implement decisions or to make progress; who will do what by when.
- *Future agenda items.*
- *Date, time, and place for next meeting.*

FIGURE 8-5

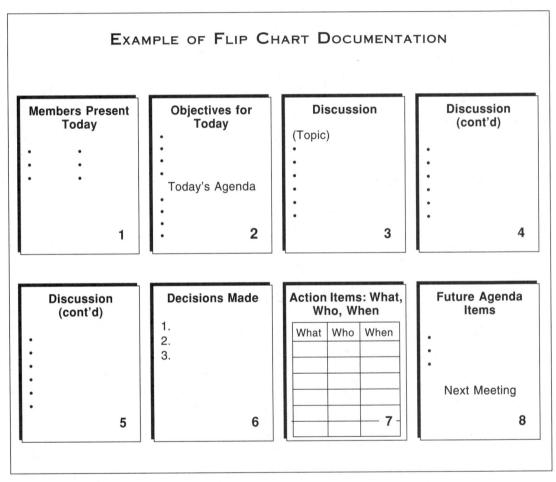

EXAMPLE OF FLIP CHART DOCUMENTATION

Members Present Today

1

Objectives for Today

Today's Agenda

2

Discussion

(Topic)

3

Discussion (cont'd)

4

Discussion (cont'd)

5

Decisions Made

1.
2.
3.

6

Action Items: What, Who, When

What	Who	When

7

Future Agenda Items

Next Meeting

8

FIGURE 8-6

EXAMPLE OF RECORDER-COMPOSED MINUTES

Meeting Record

Group: _____

Members present: _____
_____
_____

Objectives of this meeting:

Agenda:

Topic: _____

  Main points:

  Decision:

  Action items:

Topic:

  Main points:

  Decision:

  Action items:

Next meeting (date, time, and place):

_____
_____
_____

ASSIGN ACTION PLAN

Most meetings should end with an action planning process. This solidifies agreements made and starts the work process. What follows is a simplified action planning process to use when the team has only a few action steps to plan at a time:

- Ask: What are the next steps? Who's responsible? When does the action need to be completed? Who receives the completed work? Are there any actions that must be completed first? **Note:** *Only one person should be responsible for each action item. If others are involved or are giving input, indicate those as separate action items for those people.*

- Once all the actions are listed, identify which action items are dependent on others and adjust deadlines accordingly.

- Record the information on a flip chart for all to see and discuss. Someone should copy the information onto an action plan form (see Figure 8–7) and make a copy for each team member to take with him or her.

- At the next meeting get a status report on each action item. Make a new form for the action items that result from the second meeting. Do this for each meeting.

- Give each action item a *separate number* over the course of several meetings or throughout the life of the project. Each action item should keep the original number assigned to it. When it is completed, do not use that number again for subsequent action items. This helps people keep track of what has been done over time and allows for easy reference to and discussion of past and current action items.

FIGURE 8-7

ACTION PLAN CHECKLIST*

Time _____

Date _____

What?	Who?	When?

* This checklist is located in Appendix II: Checklists.

EVALUATE MEETING RESULTS

At the end of each meeting, do one of the following to evaluate your team's meeting and to target improvements:

OPTION 1

Use the *Checklist for Opening and Closing Team Meetings* (see Figure 8–3). Then ask one another the following questions:

- "How did the meeting go?"

- "What worked well that we should include next time?"

- "What should we do differently?"

Record the replies.

OPTION 2

Use the assessment entitled *Checklist for Successful Meetings*. (See Figure 8–8.)

- Each team member should complete the form.

- Have a team discussion of the results.

- Have the team devise ways to improve meetings.

OPTION 3

One team member could assume the role of process observer and give feedback on the meeting.

- Complete the *Checklist for Successful Meetings*.

- Share the observations and checklist notations with the team.

FIGURE 8-8

CHECKLIST FOR SUCCESSFUL MEETINGS*

Please answer the following questions by placing a check (✔) in the appropriate column.

Our Team

	Does Not Do	Does Sometimes	Does Consistently
Holds regular team meetings.	❑	❑	❑
Has clear meeting objective(s) or purpose.	❑	❑	❑
Has clear meeting roles (see Chapter 5, "Understanding Team Support Roles").	❑	❑	❑
Always has a meeting leader (either the team leader or the team facilitator).	❑	❑	❑
Encourages team members to suggest agenda items for upcoming meetings.	❑	❑	❑
Gives all team members advance notice of meeting time and place.	❑	❑	❑
Keeps to a scheduled beginning and ending time.	❑	❑	❑
Starts each meeting by agreeing to what will be resolved or accomplished at the meeting (the meeting purpose).	❑	❑	❑
Goes over the agenda to see if it supports the meeting objectives.	❑	❑	❑
Uses appropriate group processes for achieving the objectives.	❑	❑	❑
Posts agreed-upon team ground rules.	❑	❑	❑
Uses a skilled team facilitator for the first few meetings and for particularly difficult or involved meetings.	❑	❑	❑
Invites the appropriate people to the meeting.	❑	❑	❑
Manages the meeting time so that people are not rushed or railroaded and so that time is not wasted due to the discussion's getting off track.	❑	❑	❑
Keeps a separate list of issues or agenda items for future meetings (not appropriate for the current meeting).	❑	❑	❑
Takes time to summarize the meeting results so people know what's expected of them between meetings.	❑	❑	❑

* This checklist is located in Appendix II: Checklists.

Team Situation

A marketing staff group for worldwide design and production of electronic components had discontinued its weekly staff meetings. The meetings had been ineffective: they lasted too long; no decisions were made; and the same people did all the talking. After a few months, however, communications were breaking down, and the information loss was causing the group to become dysfunctional.

They were challenged by their human resource consultant: "How can you conduct marketing meetings all over the world, yet not make your own meetings work?" This person asked if she could observe one of their marketing sessions. She discovered the staff members were adept at using overhead transparencies but did not know how to involve the audience or lead group discussions.

Team Process

The human resource consultant offered to facilitate a few meetings with the staff to demonstrate meeting facilitation and meeting techniques. She referred them to the book *How to Make Meetings Work* by Michael Doyle and David Strauss and then demonstrated the following as discussed in various parts of this chapter:

1. **Team meeting agenda format.**

   This was done in a group brainstorming manner at the beginning and end of each meeting. At the end of the meeting, team members listed items to be included in the agenda for the next meeting. They also determined the action items that needed to be accomplished between meetings. The prioritizing and time allotments for each agenda item were left for the beginning of the next meeting and were set according to changing customer priorities.

2. **Action plan.**

   The action plan served two purposes: coordinating who should do what and ensuring attendance at the next meeting. Since the group had become unaccustomed to holding meetings, there was a lack of commitment toward participating once meetings were reenacted; members would float in and out of meetings at will. But when they were assigned action items and did not know what time

Teams in Action

their items would be discussed, members found they needed to attend and participate in the whole meeting.

3. **Flip chart documentation.**

   Flip chart recording during the session helped to move the conversation more quickly and to keep the group focused on its agenda items. The time allotment was noted on the top of the page for each action item.

TEAM RESULTS

This staff was amazed at how useful meetings could be. What had taken them many grueling hours to hash through in the past was now handled easily in two hours. They appreciated and utilized the group notes on easel paper so much that they established a "story board room" in one of their conference rooms; on the walls of this room they posted easel sheets that had information others in marketing needed to know.

This room became their means of communicating on an informal basis. Others in marketing would write questions or comments on Post-Its and place them on the sheets. Since most of the people in this department traveled extensively and were gone for periods of time, this was an effective way to transfer information.

GLOSSARY

The following glossary includes terms and processes referenced in *Teaming by Design: Real Teams for Real People.*

action plan *(n.)* a list of activities assigned during a team meeting. The list includes the activity, the responsible team member(s), and the due date.

cohesive work group *(n.)* a group that focuses on the needs of its individual members through group work.

collective wisdom *(n.)* the knowledge, experience, and information of a broad base of people.

consensus *(n.)* a situation in which everyone in the group or team fully supports a decision.

core conflict *(n.)* conflict that impedes the progress of a team from accomplishing its task(s) or reaching its goal(s).

cross-functional *(adj.)* representing multiple functions.

cross-functional team *(n.)* a team whose members represent various parts of the formal organization. It is common for this type of team to have a specific one-time assignment that addresses a broad issue, problem, or opportunity.

customer *(n.)* the end user of a product or service. Any person or entity that chooses to use a team's products or services to meet their goals.

effective organizational unit *(n.)* a team that integrates its work into the larger organization and collaborates with other teams and work units in shared teaming.

efficient work team *(n.)* a team that focuses on increasing its efficiency in accomplishing work tasks as a self-directed team.

flip chart transcription *(n.)* documentation of team meeting agendas, main points of discussion, decisions, and action items. During the meeting the flip chart sheets are recorded on and posted for all members to see. After the meeting the chart sheets are typed and distributed to all members.

goals *(n.)* specific targets that bring a team closer to realizing its mission. Goals address what the team is going to do.

group process *(n.)* activities that support the team members, the team as a whole, and the work environment.

guidelines *(n.)* the ground rules or norms designating how team members will work with one another.

independent work *(n.)* work that is produced by individual contributors, each offering a unique contribution toward achieving a shared goal.

intact team *(n.)* a permanent or existing work group that produces an identifiable product or service.

interdependence *(n.)* the state in which each team member makes individual contributions and other members depend on those contributions. The members also share work information with one another. They are accepted by and able to influence one another.

matrix *(n.)* multiple command system that includes not only a multiple command structure but also related support mechanisms and organizational culture.[1]

mission/purpose *(n.)* the desired results for team activities. The team mission or purpose identifies why the team exists.

---

[1]S. M. David & P. R. Lawrence, 1977. *Matrix.* Reading, Massachusetts: Addison-Wesley.

objectives *(n.)* detailed actions that include the resources required to achieve those actions and support team goals.

peripheral conflict *(n.)* conflict that does not significantly hinder the team's progress toward its goal.

recorder-composed documentation *(n.)* a form of documentation in which the team recorder takes notes during the meeting, writes them on flip chart paper or inputs them in a laptop computer, and then distributes them afterward in the form of "minutes."

shared responsibility *(n.)* an understanding and acceptance that responsibility for the team's purpose and goals is shared and understood by all members (rather than held solely by the manager or team leader).

shared teaming *(n.)* a way of working that involves both integrating work with team members and linking team work between and among other teams and other parts of the organization.

subject matter expert (SME) *(n.)* an individual with a specific area of expertise who is pulled into a team as a resource.

tasks *(n.)* activities required to perform the work itself; these activities are in support of the team mission.

team *(n.)* a group of individuals who share work activities and the responsibility for specific outcomes.

team charter *(n.)* a document written by team members that defines the team's mission or purpose, goals and objectives, team role, and norms or guidelines. The charter is critical to a team's success.

team facilitator *(n.)* the individual who ensures that team members participate in decision making as equals. The facilitator guides the team to recommendations made by consensus rather than by one or more dominant members.

team generalist *(n.)* a person fulfilling the requirements of a position that requires multiple activities and skills.

team goals *(n.)* specific targets that bring the team closer to realizing its mission.

team time keeper *(n.)* the individual accountable for managing the agenda. The timekeeper informs the team of time allowances and constraints.

team leader *(n.)* the individual accountable for keeping the team focused on its task. The team leader works closely with the sponsor to link the team to the larger organization.

team members *(n.)* individuals in a group who collaborate with each other and the leader to set and achieve the team's goals, to work together as a team, and to present recommendations.

team norms *(n.)* patterns, behaviors, and activities that provide ground rules or guidelines for how the team members will work with one another.

team outcomes *(n.)* the results of the team's activities— includes both services and products. Accountability for team outcomes is shared by all members.

team recorder *(n.)* team member accountable for recording the ideas and decisions of the group in team meetings.

team role *(n.)* the part the team plays in helping an organization attain its vision.

team specialist *(n.)* a person who performs specific work as an individual contributor.

team sponsor *(n.)* the individual who assumes ownership and accountability for a team's assignment and serves as a mentor to the team. The sponsor is the link to the rest of the organization.

team tasks *(n.)* activities that support getting the team's work done.

three levels of teaming *(n.)* an assessment process used to determine the degree of teaming required. The team assesses whether it is simply in need of group work, whether it needs to become a self-directed team, or whether it needs to participate in shared teaming.

work unit *(n.)* a number of subteams with different assignments and individuals performing various stages of the work.

WorkStyle Patterns™ data *(n.)* data that reveal trends for workforce preferences, work requirements, and for each of the three levels of teaming.

WorkStyle Patterns™ Inventory *(n.)* a self-scoring assessment that compares preferred and position of team WorkStyles.

APPENDIX I

RESOURCES

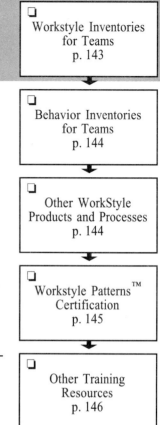

❏ Workstyle Inventories
for Teams
p. 143

❏ Behavior Inventories
for Teams
p. 144

❏ Other WorkStyle
Products and Processes
p. 144

❏ Workstyle Patterns™
Certification
p. 145

❏ Other Training
Resources
p. 146

The following Resource Appendix describes products and processes referenced in different sections of this handbook.

WORKSTYLE INVENTORIES FOR TEAMS

The McFletcher Corporation's WorkStyle Patterns™ process affirms that each employee has a preferred approach to work and each work environment requires a certain approach to attain team and organizational goals. By bringing these approaches into alignment, organizations and their teams increase efficiency and individuals enjoy greater fulfillment.

WorkStyle™ products designed specifically for teams help clarify their purpose, approach, assignments, and activities.

- The McFletcher Corporation's **WorkStyle Patterns™ Inventory (WSP™)** assesses and compares personal and position WorkStyles. It describes work activities, determines individual preferences, identifies the alignment, and compares personal and organizational stress. The Inventory is self-scoring and does not require computer analysis. It includes Profile descriptions, interpretation instructions, and self–position comparisons.

- **Team Role Assessment Inventory** identifies the overall role of a team in meeting organization or function goals. This assessment clarifies and prioritizes activities required for team projects and tasks.
- **Team Member Assignment Inventory** profiles specific team assignments and aligns them to the team role. Coupled with the *WSP™ Inventory,* this assessment enables a team to select and assign appropriate group members for team projects and assignments.
- **WorkStyle Alignment Packet 6: Teams** provides simple instructions and exercises for team members to understand the work approach required for team and individual assignments.

BEHAVIOR INVENTORIES FOR TEAMS

LIFO® Training Division

Life Orientations™ Survey

Stuart Atkins Inc.

9301 Wilshire Blvd. Suite 306

Beverly Hills, CA 90210

(213) 276–5424

Meyers-Briggs Type Indicator® (MBTI®)

Consulting Psychologists Press

P.O. Box 10096

Palo Alto, CA 94303

(415) 969–8901

Personal Profile System© (DISC®)

Performax Systems International

12755 State Highway 55

Minneapolis, MN 55441

(612) 540–5110

OTHER WORKSTYLE PRODUCTS AND PROCESSES

WSP™ products and software programs enable organizations to achieve their objectives.

- The **Employer Actual Inventory** provides organizational or customer expectations of positions.

- The **WorkStyle Alignment Packets** enable individuals and employers an opportunity to assess WSP™ information and develop action plans to increase their own productivity. Through a self-guided process with explanations, checklists, and guidelines, each packet addresses a unique aspect of work-style alignment.

- **Work Design Handbook 7** offers the why, what, and how for "reengineering" or designing the work. The handbook provides specific steps and visuals. Selected client samples are provided from McFletcher's Work Design database for benchmark comparisons.

- **WSP™ Normative Data Base Applications** measure individual and organizational performance through a normative database that answers productivity concerns. This service, available on an input-fee basis, determines accurate Profile results, compiles discrepancies and performs comparative analysis.

WORKSTYLE PATTERNS™ CERTIFICATION

WorkStyle Certification provides opportunities for transferring alignment skills into organizations.

- **WSP™ Facilitator Certification,** a requirement for those who use WSP™ inventories, offers an in-depth understanding of WSP™ content and interpretations. Certification participants learn how to apply *Teaming by Design: Real Teams for Real People* and the WSP™ in their work environment through interpreting inventory scores, training exercises, and comparing research results with organizational problems.

- *Teams in the Workplace Advanced Certification* enables organizations to design team structures, roles and tasks; to implement reward systems for both individual and team performance; and to train employees as they transition into new areas of accountability. This program is implemented with an actual team and custom designed to include the team's mission and work assignments. *Teaming by Design: Real Teams for Real People* and *Team Inventories* are included for each team member.

Other Training Resources

American Supplier Institute (ASI)
Six Parklane Blvd. Suite 411
Dearborn, MI 48126
(313) 336–8877

How to Lead Work Teams, Facilitation Skills
Rees, Fran (1991)
Pfeiffer & Company
San Diego, CA 92121
(619) 578-2042

How to Make Meetings Work
Michael Doyle & David Straus (1976)
Jove Books
New York, NY

LIFO® Training Division
Stuart Atkins Inc.
9301 Wilshire Blvd. Suite 306
Beverly Hills, CA 9021
(213) 276-5424

Meyers-Briggs Type Indicator® (MBTI®)
Consulting Psychologists Press
P.O. Box 10096
Palo Alto, CA 94303
(415) 969-8901

Personal Profile System© (DISC™)
Performax Systems International
12755 State Highway 55
Minneapolis, MN 55441
(612) 540-5110

The Secrets of a Dynamic Subordinate that Every Manager Should Know
Crockett, William J.
The Center for Applied Behavior Sciences
P.O. Box 1639
Sun City, AZ 85372

CHECKLISTS

ASSIGNMENT PLANNING CHECKLIST FOR TEAMS

When Planning Work Assignments with Other Team Members, Do We	No	Yes Sometimes	Yes Consistently
1. Specify the assignment's main **purpose?**	❏	❏	❏
2. Stress the **results** we need following completion of each assignment?	❏	❏	❏
3. Determine how the **work assignment** fits with other work being done?	❏	❏	❏
4. Clarify how the **assignment** may or may not be different from previous assignments?	❏	❏	❏
5. Provide all the **information** needed to successfully carry out the assignment?	❏	❏	❏
6. List answers to the **"what, when, who, where, how, and why"** of the assignment?	❏	❏	❏
7. Assess the **limitations** (e.g., time, cost, etc. that could affect the assignment's completion)?	❏	❏	❏
8. Provide for **contingencies** or alternate plans should difficulties arise?	❏	❏	❏
9. Reinforce **critical parts** of the assignment by checking on our work in progress and giving positive feedback?	❏	❏	❏
10. Establish **controls** with each other so we're checking on progress?	❏	❏	❏
11. **Document** our plans, process, and results for group memory and shared accountability?	❏	❏	❏
12. Arrange for **coordination** with other departments or teams who might be affected by the work assignment?	❏	❏	❏
13. Solicit **feedback** from team members to assess our shared understanding of the assignment?	❏	❏	❏
14. Arrange for **reviewing/debriefing** after the assignment is completed?	❏	❏	❏

CHECKLIST FOR A PRODUCTIVE TEAM

Please refer to this "Extent Scale Guide" in answering the following questions:

	Very Little Extent	Little Extent	Some Extent	Great Extent	Very Great Extent
1. To what extent do you enjoy performing your team activities?	1	2	3	4	5
2. To what extent do you feel a real responsibility to help your team be successful?	1	2	3	4	5
3. To what extent do you feel you are accepted as a member of your team?	1	2	3	4	5
4. To what extent do you feel you receive enough praise or recognition when a job is well done?	1	2	3	4	5
5. How receptive are people higher in the organization to team suggestions and new ideas?	1	2	3	4	5
6. Does the organization keep an open and frank flow of information about important events affecting your team?	1	2	3	4	5
7. Do other functions or teams plan and coordinate their efforts to maintain an effective flow of work activity?	1	2	3	4	5
8. Are there things about working on this team (people, policies, or conditions) that encourage you to work hard?	1	2	3	4	5
9. To what extent is the organization generally quick to accept your team's improved work methods?	1	2	3	4	5
10. Are the decisions made at those levels where the most adequate and accurate information is available?	1	2	3	4	5
11. Does the organization have a real interest in the welfare and happiness of those who work on your team?	1	2	3	4	5
12. How much does the organization try to improve working conditions for your team?	1	2	3	4	5
13. To what extent does the organization have clear-cut, reasonable goals and objectives for your team to support?	1	2	3	4	5
14. To what extent are work activities for this team sensibly organized?	1	2	3	4	5
15. How adequate is the information you get about other functions (or related teams)?	1	2	3	4	5
16. Are the equipment and resources your team has to work with adequate, efficient, and well maintained?	1	2	3	4	5

Adapted and modified for teams from Organization Dynamics, Inc., 1978.

GOALS AND OBJECTIVES CHECKLIST		
Team Goal	**Objectives to Support the Goal**	**Target Date for Completion**
1	• • • •	
2	• • • •	
3	• • • •	

THREE LEVELS OF TEAMING: CHARACTERISTICS

LEVEL A COHESIVE WORK GROUP *Group Work*	LEVEL B EFFICIENT WORK TEAM *Self-Directed Team*	LEVEL C EFFECTIVE ORGANIZATIONAL UNIT *Shared Teaming*
Most required characteristics of a cohesive work group:	*Most required characteristics of an efficient work team:*	*Most required characteristics of an effective organizational unit:*
❏ Identification first with individual work and second with that of the group.	❏ High identification with own team.	❏ More awareness of other teams; less "own team" identity.
❏ Decision-making processes with individual and group input.	❏ Decision-making process shared among team members.	❏ Decision-making process shared between teams and with other parts of the organization.
❏ Formal communication sessions for sharing of group results. Minimal requirement for informal or spontaneous communication.	❏ Extensive feedback and clarification within own team. Frequent informal or spontaneous communication.	❏ Extensive use of intra- and interteam feedback and clarification. Communication in "our organization" terms.
❏ Segregated assignments with minimal sharing of work tasks or integrating work objectives.	❏ Common knowledge base among team members with work processes and production problems.	❏ Continuous checking of other teams' progress and realignment of the work.
❏ Comfortable group atmosphere.	❏ Unity and mutual support to defend team purpose and goals. "Our team" identity.	❏ General tone is collaborative for satisfaction of everyone in the organization, "betterment of the whole."
❏ Basic respect and mutual support for individuals' knowledge and skills.	❏ Mutual respect and admiration within team for accomplishment of shared goals.	❏ Conscious effort to build trust with other teams and other parts of the organization.
❏ Synergy from group recognition of individual contributions.	❏ Synergy from feelings of winning through accomplishment of "own team" goals.	❏ Synergy from feelings of winning through goal accomplishment for the total organization.

ROLE CHECKLIST FOR THE TEAM LEADER

Please answer the following questions by placing a check (✔) in the appropriate column.

The Team Leader

	Does Not Do	Does Sometimes	Does Consistently
1. Helps the group focus and maintain its energy toward the task by:			
• Soliciting team member input on agenda items prior to meetings.	❏	❏	❏
• Preparing and distributing agenda at least two days before meetings.	❏	❏	❏
• Working with the facilitator to ensure the meeting space is free of distractions.	❏	❏	❏
• Arranging meeting room furniture to maximize communication.	❏	❏	❏
• Keeping the group on track during the meeting.	❏	❏	❏
2. Helps keep the facilitator and recorder in their respective roles by:			
• Discussing the agenda, goals and issues prior to meetings.	❏	❏	❏
• Calling upon both to perform their functions during meetings.	❏	❏	❏
3. Initiates in setting directions for the group.	❏	❏	❏
4. Clarifies organizational expectations and constraints.	❏	❏	❏
5. Provides information and opinions based upon technical knowledge but does not dominate group.	❏	❏	❏
6. Guides the group in terms of its decision making, seeking consensus-type approach.	❏	❏	❏
7. Evaluates group's progress in relation to task and gives feedback to all members.	❏	❏	❏
8. Represents the group in the larger organization.	❏	❏	❏

Adapted from Doyle and Strauss, *How to Make Meetings Work* (NY: Jove Books, 1976).

ROLE CHECKLIST FOR THE TEAM MEMBER

Please answer the following questions by placing a check (✔) in the appropriate column.

The Team Member

	Does Not Do	Does Sometimes	Does Consistently
1. Helps the team focus and maintain energy toward the task by:			
• Supporting the team's charter and mission.	❑	❑	❑
• Being present and attentive at team meetings.	❑	❑	❑
• Asking questions and seeking clarity on the task.	❑	❑	❑
• Avoiding getting stuck on own opinion or solution.	❑	❑	❑
2. Participates in all aspects of the team's work by:			
• Listening to others.	❑	❑	❑
• Offering own ideas and suggestions.	❑	❑	❑
• Volunteering to take appropriate action items.	❑	❑	❑
• Keeping others posted and informed.	❑	❑	❑
3. Supports team cohesiveness by:			
• Drawing out ideas and participation from other team members.	❑	❑	❑
• Communicating own needs, concerns, and feelings.	❑	❑	❑
• Validating other team members' needs, concerns, and feelings.	❑	❑	❑
• Helping others achieve their action items.	❑	❑	❑
• Asking for help when needed.	❑	❑	❑
4. Supports synergy and creativity by:			
• Learning creative tools and participating in creative team sessions.	❑	❑	❑
• Exploring alternatives for all decisions.	❑	❑	❑

Adapted from Doyle and Strauss, *How to Make Meetings Work* (NY: Jove Books, 1976).

ROLE CHECKLIST FOR THE TEAM FACILITATOR

Please answer the following questions by placing a check (✔) in the appropriate column.

The Team Facilitator

	Does Not Do	Does Sometimes	Does Consistently
1. Helps each member of the team to fully participate by:			
• Gaining membership in the team.	❏	❏ .	❏
• Developing influence in the team.	❏	❏	❏
• Understanding the precise nature of the team's task assignment.	❏	❏	❏
• Developing a set of team operating norms that encourage individual participation.	❏	❏	❏
2. Makes observations and suggestions regarding the team's methods and procedures.	❏	❏	❏
3. Stays neutral with regard to opinions and ideas about the team's task by returning questions of that nature to team members.	❏	❏	❏
4. Protects members and their ideas from attack.	❏	❏	❏
5. Acts as a model for team members of how to be a productive member.	❏	❏	❏
6. Gives feedback to entire team and individual members as to how they are doing in their process.	❏	❏	❏
7. Gives support to the team recorder.	❏	❏	❏
8. Evaluates and provides feedback to team with regard to its development as a team.	❏	❏	❏
9. Helps with coordination of team's relations to outside elements.	❏	❏	❏
10. Coordinates pre- and postmeeting logistics.	❏	❏	❏

Adapted from Doyle and Strauss, *How to Make Meetings Work* (NY: Jove Books, 1976).

ROLE CHECKLIST FOR THE TEAM RECORDER

Please answer the following questions by placing a check (✔) in the appropriate column.

The Team Recorder

	Does Not Do	Does Sometimes	Does Consistently
1. Captures basic ideas on large sheets of paper in full view of the team:			
• Refrains from editing or paraphrasing.	❑	❑	❑
• Uses the words of the member speaking.	❑	❑	❑
• Records enough of the speaker's ideas so they can be understood later.	❑	❑	❑
2. Remains neutral by:			
• Refraining from contributing own ideas.	❑	❑	❑
• Keeping pace with the team. (If the recorder gets lost or does not hear, that is OK. He or she may stop the team and ask people to repeat or slow down.)	❑	❑	❑
• Supporting and following the facilitator.	❑	❑	❑
• Listening for key words versus writing every word.	❑	❑	❑
• Making corrections nondefensively.	❑	❑	❑
3. Provides a visual team memory by:			
• Printing/writing legibly with letters about an inch and a half high.	❑	❑	❑
• Writing fast.	❑	❑	❑
• Concerning self with content; not afraid of misspelling.	❑	❑	❑
• Abbreviating words to keep up with conversation.	❑	❑	❑
• Varying colors; using colors to highlight, divide ideas, underline.	❑	❑	❑
• Varying the size of writing/printing.	❑	❑	❑
• Using outline form.	❑	❑	❑
• Using stars, arrows, numbers, dots, and so forth.	❑	❑	❑
• Numbering all sheets.	❑	❑	❑

Adapted from Doyle and Strauss, *How to Make Meetings Work* (NY: Jove Books, 1976).

REVERSE MIRRORING VALUES WORKSHEET

"How we _____ see ourselves"

"How we see _____"

_____

_____

_____

_____

_____

_____

_____

_____

1	2
3	4

"How we think _____ see(s) us"

"How _____ think(s) we see them"

_____

_____

_____

_____

_____

_____

_____

_____

CHECKLIST FOR DETERMINING FACILITATOR REQUIREMENTS

Place a check (✔) in the boxes appropriate for your team.

When to use a meeting facilitator

❑ For the first few meetings when your team has to get organized, get team members acquainted, and establish the team's charter.

❑ When the meeting involves dealing with a lot of data, opinions, and viewpoints, or when there is likely to be substantial disagreement, conflict, or confusion.

❑ When consensus on an important decision needs to be reached.

❑ When team-meeting ground rules and meeting behaviors need to be discussed, or when the productivity of your team needs to be discussed and evaluated.

❑ When your team needs someone who has knowledge of group or technical processes.

❑ When the team leader and/or team members have difficulty listening to one another, keeping a balance of participation, or involving everyone in decision making.

When *not* to use a meeting facilitator

❑ For every team meeting, once you are organized and your charter is set.

❑ For short update meetings or meetings of a more presentational nature.

❑ For a mature team—one that is in the *performing* stage (except on occasion, for difficult meetings).

❑ When someone on your team can act as the facilitator— remain neutral, get balanced participation, and so forth.

SUPPLIES, FACILITIES AND EQUIPMENT CHECKLIST

Place a check (✔) in the box once you have located an item.

You will need the following for most of your team meetings and other work:

❑ Flip chart easel and paper. (White board space is adequate for most team meetings.)

❑ Marking pens (be sure there are plenty)

Water-based (don't bleed through onto walls).

Use those meant for paper (not white boards).

Have three or four different colors for highlighting, organizing.

Mr. Sketch (scented) are easy to use; El Marko makes a good water-based pen.

Use darkest colors for main text, lighter/brighter colors for highlighting.

❑ Pencils.

❑ Scissors.

❑ Masking tape (for posting flip charts on walls).

❑ Overhead projector, projector pens, transparencies, and screen. (White wall space can be used in place of screen.)

❑ Blank forms (such as action planning forms, meeting evaluation forms, etc.).

❑ Note paper.

❑ Post It notes.

❑ *Teaming by Design* (for reference).

❑ Copies of appropriate documentation:

Action items from previous meeting.

Information, data, and anything else that team members will need to keep informed and make decisions.

❑ Meeting space (comfortable and adequate).

CHECKLIST FOR OPENING AND CLOSING TEAM MEETINGS

Place a check (✔) in the boxes appropriate for your team.

How to open a team meeting

❑ Start on time.

❑ Introduce any meeting guests.

❑ Review the charter, mission, and guidelines.

❑ Post meeting objectives/purpose and the agenda.

❑ Check to see if everyone agrees to the purpose and the agenda.

❑ Add agenda items as necessary, but keep meeting time limit in mind. Begin list of agenda items for future meetings.

❑ Review meeting ground rules the team has agreed upon.

❑ Announce who will be the recorder.

How to close a team meeting

❑ Allow 15–20 minutes to close the meeting (longer for lengthy, involved meetings).

❑ Post and review all decisions made and check for buy-in and understanding.

❑ Ask, "What action items have we agreed to / do we need to agree to?"

❑ Post all action items with **who** will do **what** by **when.** Check for buy-in.

❑ Set the next meeting time and date if possible.

❑ Review the collected list of issues and agenda items for future meetings. Get team's input on important items for upcoming meetings.

❑ Thank people for coming.

❑ End on time.

❑ From time to time, evaluate your team's meeting using the Checklist for Successful Meetings.

ACTION PLAN CHECKLIST

Time _____

Date _____

What?	Who?	When?

CHECKLIST FOR SUCCESSFUL MEETINGS

Please answer the following questions by placing a check (✔) in the appropriate column.

Our Team

	Does Not Do	Does Sometimes	Does Consistently
Holds regular team meetings.	❏	❏	❏
Has clear meeting objective(s) or purpose.	❏	❏	❏
Has clear meeting roles (see Chapter 5, Understanding Team Support Roles).	❏	❏	❏
Always has a meeting leader (either the team leader or the team facilitator).	❏	❏	❏
Encourages team members to suggest agenda items for upcoming meetings.	❏	❏	❏
Gives all team members advance notice of meeting time and place.	❏	❏	❏
Keeps to a scheduled beginning and ending time.	❏	❏	❏
Starts each meeting by agreeing to what will be resolved or accomplished at the meeting (the meeting purpose).	❏	❏	❏
Goes over the agenda to see if it supports the meeting objectives.	❏	❏	❏
Uses appropriate group processes for achieving the objectives.	❏	❏	❏
Posts agreed-upon team ground rules.	❏	❏	❏
Uses a skilled team facilitator for the first few meetings and for particularly difficult or involved meetings.	❏	❏	❏
Invites the appropriate people to the meeting.	❏	❏	❏
Manages the meeting time so that people are not rushed or railroaded and so that time is not wasted due to the discussion's getting off track.	❏	❏	❏
Keeps a separate list of issues or agenda items for future meetings (not appropriate for the current meeting).	❏	❏	❏
Takes time to summarize the meeting results so people know what's expected of them between meetings.	❏	❏	❏

Index

R

S

T

Other Books of interest to you from Irwin Professional Publishing . . .

DIVERSE TEAMS AT WORK

Capitalizing on the Power of Diversity

Lee Gardenswartz and Anita Rowe

Provides guidelines for building and managing teams that have members from a variety of backgrounds. Includes tips on how to resolve conflicts, solve problems, and make decisions as a highly diverse group. (175 pages)
ISBN: 0-7863-0425-1

GLOBAL SOLUTIONS FOR TEAMS

Moving from Collision to Collaboration

Sylvia B. Odenwald

Includes groundbreaking strategies that multinational workgroups can use to overcome distance as well as cultural differences to help better accomplish common goals and develop higher productivity. (195 pages)
ISBN: 0-7863-0476-6

LEADING TEAMS

Mastering the New Role

John H. Zenger, Ed Musselwhite, Kathleen Hurson, and Craig Perrin

Focuses specifically on the role of the leader as the key to long-term success, showing how managers can carve an enduring, vital position for themselves in a team environment. (275 pages)
ISBN: 1-55623-894-0

Also available in fine bookstores and libraries everywhere.

For more information about McFletcher's Team products, processes, data base research and consulting services, contact:

- The McFletcher Corporation -
10617 N. Hayden Road Suite #103
Scottsdale, Arizona 85260
Tel: (602) 991-9497
Fax: (602) 448-7955

Please indicate areas of interest:

Team Products for:

___ Facilitation

___ WorkStyle Preferences and Alignment

___ Data Base for Teams

Consulting Services for:

___ Organizational Systems/Structures

___ Work Design Technology

___ Cultural Integration

___ Participatory Environment

___ Individual/ Career Development

Name _____

Title _____

Organization _____

Address _____

_____

Telephone (____)_____

Facsimile (____)_____

There are _____ employees in my organization and _____ employees at my site.

Type of business _____

The McFletcher Corporation *For immediate reply please fax your information to (602) 948-7955.*

For more information about McFletcher's Team products, processes, data base research and consulting services, contact:

- The McFletcher Corporation -
10617 N. Hayden Road Suite #103
Scottsdale, Arizona 85260
Tel: (602) 991-9497
Fax: (602) 448-7955

Please indicate areas of interest:

Name _____

Title _____

Organization _____

Address _____

Telephone ( ) _____

Facsimile ( ) _____

There are _____ employees in my organization and _____ employees at my site.

Type of business _____

Team Products for:
___ Facilitation
___ WorkStyle Preferences and Alignment
___ Data Base for Teams

Consulting Services for:
___ Organizational Systems/Structures
___ Work Design Technology
___ Cultural Integration
___ Participatory Environment
___ Individual/ Career Development

The McFletcher Corporation *For immediate reply please fax your information to (602) 948-7955.*